JUST A TICK

Harold Donnell

AuthorHouse™ UK Ltd.
500 Avebury Boulevard
Central Milton Keynes, MK9 2BE
www.authorhouse.co.uk
Phone: 08001974150

© *2009 Harold Donnell. All rights reservved.*

No part of this book may be reproduced, stored in a retrieval system, or transmitted by any means without the written permission of the author.

First published by AuthorHouse 9/15/2009

ISBN: 978-1-4389-6118-7 (sc)

This book is printed on acid-free paper.

ABOUT THE AUTHOR

1945 - Myself and wife to be, Dorothy

Born Harold Ifor Donnell in Caerwys, Flintshire, North Wales on 20th July 1920, Harold was affectionately known as Lal to family and friends but was later to become known as Don by his friends and colleagues.

He married Dorothy Frances Margaret Wood on 30th March 1946 and they set-up home in Sandycroft, Flintshire. In 1965, four girls and three boys later, they moved to Buckley where Don now lives. Sadly, Dot passed away in November 2007 but Don still has the support of his family comprising at the present time of three sons, five daughters, sixteen grandchildren and eleven great-grandchildren.

In his retirement, Don enjoys researching most subjects and giving talks to local groups in the Chester, Wrexham, Mold, Ruthin, Northop and Deeside areas. At the time of writing he is the president of the Buckley Historical Society. He is an Elder at St John's United Reformed Church in Buckley.

Foreword

In compiling this publication my objective was to contemplate the vast array of memories that I accumulated in this ever-changing world, since I first saw the light of day, in Water Street Caerwys, on the 20th of July 1920. At the very outset of the project, it dawned on me that I am indeed a very privileged and fortunate individual. I am <u>privileged</u> in that I have been blessed with quite a good memory and <u>fortunate</u> in that within the brief period of my lifetime we have probably seen more sweeping changes in the history of mankind than during the previous one thousand years.

My early recollections of the 1920's was of a country very much adhering to Victorian standards, without a doubt my primary school training in Hawarden clearly reflected that period. There was no doubt in anyone's mind that the cane ruled! Lest we get the wrong impression however, there was no cruelty involved, the cane was there simply as a deterrent. On reflection it was very rarely used and even then purely as a last resort. I feel that this strict upbringing instilled in us youngsters the art of self-discipline and respect, respect for others and particularly for our elders. Who can argue that the formula of these two qualities is the contributory factor in the moulding of character?

During my lifetime I have witnessed a transition from a world of largely horse drawn transport, the introduction of the first motorcar to our village, then to a society where most families possess at least two motorcars. I have seen at first hand the demise of our wonderful canal system, and subsequently the rise and the hay-day of the Steam Railways, followed by their decline, as branch lines and small stations were closed, due to the dominance of the road transport. World commerce in the 1920's and 30's was mostly conducted by sea, mighty cargo and passenger vessels were the norm, the latter today are big tourist businesses and the former has largely been superseded by the massive expansion of air transport. In the 20th century we witnessed that "Giant Leap for Mankind" in the successful moon landings and must wonder at what aspect of the space exploration will be observed before the closing of the 21st century.

In today's supermarket world the mighty computer and the ever-present mobile phone, control our very existence. I wonder, as we race into the future with this ever improving wonderful technology, do we ever pause to compare these man made achievements to the God given computer, that we all possess; the human mind? We have the ability, at the blink of an eye, to recall, in vivid detail, many thousands of memories, all constantly held in storage. It is a sad fact however, that very few of us ever bother to leave record of that wonderful collection, and as we pass on, so our memories go with us. As we travel through life and observe its human comings and goings the realization dawns that we are indeed just "a candle in the wind", our tiny and insignificant span, when compared to the massive clock of eternity is what I have entitled my modest contribution "Just a Tick". However, as this publication covers merely the first 25 years of my life, maybe "Just a Fraction" would be more appropriate!

How fortunate are we who have been endowed with a good memory, I feel fortunate indeed to be so blessed. The ability to review a lifespan of 88 years with some clarity is a gift for which I am eternally grateful. The human lifespan allotted to us can quite simply be summed up by the title I have given to my recollections, "Just a Tick". In our youth we rather foolishly consider ourselves to be a somewhat permanent fixture. With advancing years however, we begin to contemplate this wonderful earth of which we are a part, and try in vain to understand the vastness of the universe and space. Where does it all begin and end? In older age we come to realise how insignificant we really are. The reference to "A Worms Eye View" is also, in my case, appropriate I think, because, ever since I first saw the light of day in Caerwys on July 20th 1920, I have felt that was my station. Not, may I add, do I consider that view of the world at all detrimental, as a friend of mine once put it, some years ago, "You get the best view of all from the bottom rung of the ladder, you can see all the arse holes above you!" When studying the family tree on both my father and mother's side, a link with aristocracy can be detected, but those days had long gone,

In my references to the 20's and 30's, long before the introduction of social services and security, the only form of help for the working class people was provided by independent societies, who for a few coppers per week, would provide small limited financial help for families in dire need. One such a society was the Order of Rechabites, this order had been formed in 1835 and based its beliefs on the teaching of RECHAB (mentioned in the book of Kings) who "abstained from strong drink" and therefore I am proud to record that our family were members of this society, and believe in total abstinences. The gentlemen who was representative of this society in our village of Mancot, was very well known as "Davis the Rechabite". When at the outset of hostilities in 1939, Mr. Davies learned that I had volunteered to join the armed forces; he invited me to his home to view his treasured photo albums. This beautiful collection he had taken during his service in the First World War, he had been an officer in the Royal Artillery. He had seen action in Allenby's Middle East Army, during the struggle to exclude the Turkish Ottoman Empire from the Holy Land, the same campaign in which Colonel Lawrence (of Arabia) had been involved. I was so impressed with what I saw, and when Mr. Davies' advised me by saying, "Take up photography son, it will keep you out of mischief", I did just that. So began my long love affair with that hobby (albeit as an amateur) and I sincerely trust that my efforts with my little box camera will help to enhance the telling of my story.

A great deal of my narrative covers my view of the Second World War and there can be no doubt that the years 1935 to 1945 were probably the most vital of the twentieth century, years that I feel, changed the outlook of mankind for ever. My detailed account of that period does not in any way mean that I endorse, or glorify the use of military force and violence. Like anyone who has been involved in military conflict, I realize that warlike confrontation achieves absolutely nothing, in the final analysis there are no winners; hence I suppose, Mr. Davies' chosen route, to keep folk on the straight and narrow. In 1939 our country confronted a terrible dilemma, faced with constant humiliation and threat of military action by Germany, Italy and Japan, the question was, did we stand up to them, or merely submit? If the latter had happened, what kind of society would we part of today? As a country, we did not want to be involved in a war which we could ill afford, certainly did not want, and definitely were not prepared for, up to that time everyone had passionately believed that the Great War was the war to end all wars.

When however firm leadership was established and the clarion call by Winston Churchill, we young men of the time felt rightly proud to rally to our country's defense. It was a time of extreme danger and the very existence of our nation, and way of life was at stake, a time when people from all walks of life were thrown together into a common melting pot. The comradeship shared by all in the armed forces during the war years, was truly unbelievable.

My recollections of those vital years are not viewed from some type of lofty perch, from which I could observe an overall picture, but rather through the eyes of an ordinary serviceman. Maybe we could have rightly referred to it as "a worms eye view", recording very mundane day-to-day events. I recall the words of a pundit of the time, "active service comprises of 99% boredom and 1% action". Maybe I can count myself fortunate in getting an overall view, in that my service encompassed experience as an airman, soldier and sailor. Of the few short war years that I had, it must be said, "dire necessity was the mother of intervention". Both sides in the conflict had assembled the world's leading scientists for technical development of their respective war machines. During that brief period, advancements were made, that in the normal course of events would possibly taken many decades to achieve, some maybe along an entirely different route or probably not at all!

We witnessed the desperate fight to harness atomic energy, this was a crucial struggle, because which ever way the pendulum swung would mean success or disaster for either side, the debate still rages today as to whether that development has been a force for good or evil to mankind. Today we are reaping the fruit of the seeds sown by pioneers of jet and rocket propulsion. Of course, in those far off days, the very conduct of the war was dependant on communication by Morse code, produced by radio. In that field the constant fight for the development, and the cracking of codes led eventually to the invention of the computer with its tremendous potential for the future. In my memoirs I have endeavored, honestly and to the best of my ability to portray events and happenings of more than 60 years ago. If my mind has played tricks, and anything I have recorded proves to be in any way erroneous, then I offer my apology. I sincerely trust that you will enjoy your read.

Acknowledgements

Following our marriage, on my discharge from the forces, my wife Dot and I were fortunate to have been blessed with a large and very loving family and over the years of their upbringing it has always been my delight to tell them stories, plucked at random from my treasure chest of memories. It was during a family get together some years ago, that my youngest son Geraint said to me, "Why don't you put all your stories down in writing Dad". I began the endeavor on 30th July 2007.

I am deeply grateful to Geraint for that simple question, as it gave me the incentive to drive along the route I now pursue. The compiling of this little collection of stories would not have been possible without the help and encouragement of my "computer wise" family and I am very appreciative of their enthusiasm.

The task undertaken by my eldest Pat, in typing, editing and proof reading my hastily hand written notes, must indeed have been a daunting one despite assurances that it was a labour of love. She had some help from her son Lee and her brother Geraint and they are all due my eternal thanks for their hard work. Most of the photographs included were taken by myself and showed their age but Pat managed to bring them back to life using her computer skills to enhance them.

Harold Donnell

Many thanks are also extended to the Flintshire Records Office, in Hawarden for their kind permission to use photographs of the Reverend Canon Drew and my old school.

I must also thank all friends for their photographic donations, in particular Ron Lammond for the school gardeners picture and that of Mr Crowther's bus.

Thanks also to the custodians of Beeston Castle for permitting me to use extracts from their Guide Book, of the authors impression of the time of Prince Edward, later to be King Edward I.

My search for photographs led Pat onto the Internet and as a result I would like to thank Vicky Perfect for e-mailing photographs of Courtaulds and a big thank you to the web site www.cyber-heritage.co.uk for allowing us to use photographs of HMS Thetis and HMS Thunderbolt.

Chapter 1

At First Glance

I was introduced to this world in a small cottage in Water Street, where my Mum and Dad were struggling to rear a young family, Dad had just returned from Service in the 'World War', to a country "fit for heroes", as they had been told, only to discover that the family business, the paper mill at Afonwen, where he had held a staff position, had ceased to trade, consequently he was left destitute. In desperation my father, through contact with old comrades from the Royal Welch Fusiliers, managed to find employment at the power station in Queensferry, an ex-government armaments factory. The power station had been taken over by the Chester Corporation to provide electricity for the city (this was before the days of the grid system), it was a coal fired station, and dad accepted the position of a stoker in the boiler house, this was a dirty and very hard job which must have demanded a great deal of courage. He used to cycle every day from Caerwys! For a seven-day week, on a shift system, he received the princely weekly wage of £2-10shillings, which equates to £2.50 in today's money. It was during this time that Dad had an experience, which does not fall to many of us; he encountered "The Ghost of the Mold-Denbigh Road". His story, as he recounted it to me some years later, went as follows-:

Harold Donnell

One Winters morning he had left Caerwys at about 4:30am to start work on his 6 'til 2 shift and as he was passing the Sarn Mill near Nannerch, he saw crossing the road before him, a strange, rather misty figure, this appeared to be an old lady, in grey Victorian clothes, with a hood covering her head. He rang his bell, but the figure continued crossing the road, but what made Dad's hair stand on end, was the fact that the figure made no noise, and rather than walking, seemed to be gliding along. In terror he slammed on his brakes, and in swerving to avoid the figure, fell off his machine, imagine his bewilderment when on picking himself up, there was nothing to be seen! This apparition has been seen on many occasions, and has been featured in a book by the author Richard Holland entitled 'Ghosts of Clwyd'. This experience may have influenced Dad into getting living quarters nearer his work!! So, in January 1922, soon after the birth of my younger sister Glenys, the family obtained the tenancy of an ex government house in Mancot Way in the village of Mancot Royal. This was within walking distance of the power station; the rent was 7 shillings and 6 pence (approx. 37p) per week. My two elder brothers, Gerald, who was 16 years old and Glyn, 13 years, decided to 'stay put' in their native Caerwys. Both of course were Welsh speaking, and probably dreaded the thought of moving to the English speaking Deeside. Mr Jones, Marion Farm, took in Gerald as a "working son" and Glyn opted to stay on with the Williams family.

So the divided family that settled in 78 Mancot Way comprised, Mum, Dad, elder sister Eileen, who was then 9 years old, myself, then aged 2 years and Glenys, who was a babe in arms. Joan was born at home in 1925 and I recall that neighbours Mrs Halliwell and Mrs Smith helped with the delivery. From the outset our existence was spartan, but these of course were the days of the Great Depression. Everyone in the village was on the same level, most were families of ex-servicemen who were in the same predicament as dad, and life was hard, yes! We all really did have a "Worms Eye View".

Amazingly, my first recollection of Mancot, which I clearly remember, was soon after our arrival. I remember being wrapped up warm, and placed in an old wooden pushchair, to be taken for a walk by Eileen and Hilda Halliwell, the next-door neighbours daughter. We had only gone a few hundred yards when a startled horse came galloping towards us. As the girls screamed and ran, the animal leaped over my pushchair, knocking it, and me, into the gutter. That event has always been with me, and probably accounts for the fact that ever since, I have had a fear of horses, and especially of their hooves.

Other vivid memories I have are of long walks down to the River Dee. Dad took me onto the old Victoria Jubilee Bridge, a rickety old cast iron structure, it had just been repaired and strengthened, and was to be tested by several fully loaded Castle Fire Brick steam wagons, crossing over one at a time, from the tollgate. A footpath was cantilevered off the main bridge, and Dad insisted on standing over centre stream as the wagons passed, I recall being scared to Death, because the whole structure shook like a leaf. That old bridge was replaced in 1926 by what we now call "The Blue Bridge" and I think, not a moment too soon! I feel sure that had they continued using the old bridge it would eventually have collapsed.

From the Bridge, looking downstream in the direction of Shotton and "Hawarden Bridge", the old ferry had been abandoned on the bank of the river (we children used to climb on it to play). Dad explained to me that, as a young boy, he had crossed the river on this ferry, with his father, as they travelled by pony and trap from the family home, Ty'n-y-Caeau, in Nannerch, to visit friends and family in Wallasey. Looking upstream, near where the "Blue Bridge" was later built, were jetties at the end of the old colliery tramway, and quite a large ship building yard, this was owned by Abdelah & Mitchell and was active into the 1930's. I recall being taken by Dad again, to see the launching of the last large Paddle Steamer built there, and what an impressive sight that was, I can still picture the mighty splash as the ship was launched sideways.

Some years later, after the demolition of the old bridge, we went there to see the new bridge opened to allow the passage of one of the large grain elevators, built by Crighton of Saltney, this was towed by two tugs to Liverpool, where they were used in the docks, prior to the arrival, unloading grain from a ship, manually had taken upwards of a week. Thanks to the expertise of James Crighton, this could now be achieved in a day.

A little further upstream, at the jetty of the "Black Works" (Midland Tar distillers Ltd.), we would find the 'Water Witch' moored, this was a little tanker, which plied between the Chester gasworks and Queensferry, to supply the works with its raw material, the skipper of that vessel was an old army pal of Dads, so whenever we passed by we would always hop aboard to enjoy a cuppa in his galley, needless to say, the old vessel was liberally coated in tar, inside and out! And I can well remember Dad and I getting a good 'telling off' from Mam, when we returned home with tar on our trousers! She got rid of the offending marks by rubbing Butter on them, and then throwing our trousers in the Dolly Tub. (we were lucky we didn't follow them)

A further mention should be made here of Crighton's shipyard in Saltney, James Crighton was a wonderful engineer and Businessman, when the railway was built alongside his yard, he took full advantage, being the Pioneer of Prefabrication, he would build a ship, number every plate and fixture, and then dismantle the vessel for transportation by rail to all parts of the world, he also played a major role in the development of Saltney and its social life, building houses and recreational facilities for his workers.

By mid 1924 the time had arrived for me to be sent to school, that of course meant English school as there was no Welsh tuition at all on Deeside at that time, so one Monday morning in July I was taken "up the hill" by mum to the Infants School, which is now the church hall and was adjacent to the tithe barn. I was left in the tender care of Miss Massey and how well I remember giving vent to my feelings at being abandoned!! The little Infants school consisted of three classes standard 1 Miss Massey, standard 2 Miss Gratton, and standard 3 Miss Sillars, the head mistress. I entered that school at the tender age of 4 years and remained there until the age of 7. When it was time to go to the 'big' school, Canon Drew, we youngsters used to walk between Mancot and Hawarden, no taxis or school Buses in those days! We thought nothing of it, and I suppose that in the long term the exercise was very beneficial to us all.

Back now to my native Mancot; the pace of life in the 20's was indeed casual, we had no money for it to be otherwise and men using a horse and cart made all deliveries. One in particular which I remember was a Mr Barns, who regularly delivered BUCKLEY Pottery, Mum bought a lovely china tea set from him, on the never-never, but I cannot ever remember it being used, it was always in the china cabinet on display!

Another regular horse drawn delivery wagon operating at that time was the LMS vehicle. This was pulled by a magnificent Shire horse and driven by a Mr Joseph Ellis of Sandycroft. This operated from the sidings at Queensferry station, delivering goods throughout Deeside. Mr Ellis was a large pompous man, resplendent in his railway uniform, a fine watch and chain in his waistcoat and highly polished leggings and boots. He was a leading member of our Wesleyan chapel and may I add in all walks of life a very imposing figure.

My dad, who always kept a good kitchen garden, had an excellent arrangement with the arrival of this rig, always keeping a bucket and shovel by the back door. Whenever he saw Mr Ellis approaching the shout would go up, "Lal, Ceffyl Mawr!"[1] This was the signal for me to follow the big horse, to collect any droppings for use on the garden; they were, of course considerable!

In the very early 20's there were very few motor vehicles in the village, one of which was a beautiful old solid-tyred charabanc, now known as a coach, which had highly polished brass fittings. This was owned by Abe Lloyd and kept in the Old Fire Station, which for a while he ran as a garage. Later it was taken over by Billy Hughes, my schoolmate Ken's father, who developed it into a very successful grocery business.

At that time there were also two model T Ford lorries in the village. These were the proud possessions of our two coal merchants, Mr Bert Catherall and Mr Brown. I also recall seeing an ancient motorbike and sidecar owned by Mr Vyse who ran a newspaper round from his

---

1   Lal was my pet name and Ceffyl Mawr is Welsh for Big Horse

home. Each morning he would set off early to collect his papers from Hawarden railway station and then on his return journey he would "cruise" all the way back to Mancot without having to switch on the engine. Now that is an early example of fuel economy for you!

It may be as well, at this point, to return to our new home village, to recall many of the characters in our little community. Many were Welsh speaking, and as mam had become a member of the Wesleyan Methodist Chapel at the Pentre, we kiddies were introduced to that Sunday school. The hymn singing there was wonderful, being accompanied on a Harmonium played by Mr. Charles of Queensferry. I remember being fascinated by the male voices of Mr. Hughes, the coalman from Queensferry, Mr. Morris of 'Morris and Jones' the confectioners also of Queensferry, Mr Joseph Ellis of Sandycroft, who was the delivery man for LMS and had a magnificent Shire horse and wagon, he had a wonderful bass voice, and finally, Mr. Prydderch of Mancot, with a beautiful tenor voice. Three families who were very faithful members of that little chapel were the Curtis, Hughes and Jones' of the Blackwork's cottages at Queensferry; they used to fill a few pews.

Our little Chapel, in the Lane, had been constructed on this site in the 19th century, being relocated from its original situation, near the river's bank at Queensferry. This had been behind Abdulah and Mitchell's boatyard and near the Blackwork's Cottages, so obviously our friends the Curtis', Hughes' and Jones' ancestors had been founder members. In the 1920's the old building was still in good order, quite a tidy one at that but after ceasing to be a place of worship it had been converted into a sailors rest home. When our parents went to visit our 'Blackworks' friends we children used to play around the old sailors home and peep through the high fence at the work going on in the shipyard.

Our chapel was situated in what we called First Pentre, and from there, Mancot represented a horseshoe shape, going up Mancot Lane to 'Old Mancot' and then down Hawarden Way through Mancot Royal to the 'Second' Pentre. So I think it a good idea to *walk* that horseshoe as I try to bring to mind many of the characters that made up the Community in those days.

Just around the corner from our Chapel was a small subsidiary of Hawarden Parish Church, this had been constructed of corrugated iron and was known to everyone locally as the 'Tin Tabernacle". The custodians were Mr. Bellis and his two sisters who lived on the premises and across the road from them was a butchers shop owned by Mr. Hughes. Directly opposite Mancot Lane was Chemistry Lane and during the 19th and early 20th centuries there had been a chemical factory there. What they produced I am not sure, but also on the site was a small factory, which produced pearl buttons, that was before the days of plastic! Apparently these buttons were manufactured from animal bones obtained from local abattoirs.

Near the old factory site was a square of very primitive thatched cottages, and there lived the notorious Evans family, known to one and all in the vicinity as "Chester Jacks". Now they were a family who knew how to look after themselves! Further down that lane of course was the power station previously the old munitions works where dad now worked. Retracing our steps now to Mancot Lane, on the left were a row of houses known as Chemistry Row; and next to them a row of small buildings, which I think had some connection with the old chemistry works. Two of these buildings had been turned into quite successful businesses, first Mrs. Butlers chip shop, always a busy little place, but the Butler family actually lived near us in Mancot Way. I recall that often, when we children went by her shop, Mrs Butler could be heard talking in a loud, rather high pitched voice to her customers, so we used to shout "Pretty Pol, Pretty Pol", and run!

Another of these small buildings was converted into a very tidy little ladies hairdressers shop; Billy Roberts, a very likeable person, ran this and my elder Sister Eileen had a regular hair do there. Coming back now to Chester Road; on the corner, was Frank Jones' grocers shop, but I'm sure that even in those days, Frank was eyeing the opposition, because not far away was the Pentre Co-Op, and at Queensferry, Irwins, those firms of course were the pioneers of our modern super market chains.

Harold Donnell

We now proceed up our 'Mancot Horseshoe', where, for the first two or three hundred yards were open fields, used in those days by two local farmers, "Gagga" Wainwright, and Charlie Wright for grazing their cattle. The first residence we come to, on the left, was the newly built home of the Price family, they were of Welsh stock, and Mr. Price had built that beautiful house single-handed. Mr Price's children, Gerald, Cyril and Mary all came to our school at Hawarden, and I remember the one memorable feature of Mr. Price's character was that he had a very short fuse, but more of that later! Now we come to the houses that were referred to as "The Royal", they were government built houses, constructed during the First World War, to house the workers from the nearby munitions works. In 1916 the new development had been visited by King George V and Queen Mary, during their inspection of the munitions factory, when on their way to Hawarden as guests of the Gladstones, hence the title "Royal".

We come first to "The Square", here the houses had been built around a recreational grass square, obviously a children's' play area. On the lane end of The Square, a long workshop had been erected; this was for estate maintenance and Mr. Hooper, the estate manager, used to operate from here. We used to gaze through the windows in wonder, at the lovely machines in there. One of the families I particularly remember in The Square was the Roberts' family; the sons Ian and Roy went to school with me. During the war Ian joined the RAF like myself, but he had endured many years of captivity by the Japanese. Thankfully, being a tough Mancot lad, he survived.

Passing Crossways, on our left, we next come to a small cottage owned by yet another Price family, one of their married daughters, Mrs. Marsden, was our next-door neighbour. This cottage had originally been the engine house for the Mancot colliery, which was situated on the opposite side of the lane. Mr. Price was a likeable old character; I recall his smiling face with a beautifully trimmed beard, and the resplendent gold watch and chain in his waistcoat. He had a wonderful big garden, and always had time for a chat and to give friendly advice. Next to the Price's house we come to two small cottages on the lane side occupied by the Shaw and Walls families, one of the Shaws' daughters, Winnie, later became prominent in the nursing profession.

As we progress, we see the fields on the left, which were later, developed by Ben Williams, a local Builder. Passing Colliery Lane and its small farm on the corner, we pass a row of small cottages where the Watt and Westhead families lived and, going up the hill, arrive at Charlie Wright's farm on the corner of Cottage Lane. That corner always seemed to be ankle deep in cow manure, it was a dairy farm, but Tom Ankers, who ran the farm for Charlie, always seemed to be in his element in it! Around the corner lived a wonderful old man, we called him 'Bobby' Hall, he was a retired policeman who carried out the job of roadman for the Council. He used to go on duty on a lovely old three-wheeled bike, always very slowly, and with a large scythe swung over his shoulder, you had to give him a wide berth! His two sons later ran a very successful coal business on Deeside. Also on the corner was a sweet shop run by Mr. Jones, and directly opposite, the 'White Bear', the public house that was managed for many years by Marcus Roberts and his wife. On our left now is Walnut Cottage, a lovely little stone building, home to the Hughes family. Mr. and Mrs. Hughes always sat outside watching the world go by, but the one outstanding feature for me was Mr. Hughes' lovely big bike. He kept it in immaculate condition, always well oiled, it had a three-speed gear, and I always recall the very pleasing tick-tick sound as he slowly rode by.

Following the lane we now go up a small rise and come to the post office on our left, run by Mr. and Mrs. Ellis, and directly across the road is Parish's farm, another dairy farm. Further along on our left, we see a row of small single story cottages, in one of these my old school pal Bill Cornford was brought up. Adjacent to these, and on the site where Eric Cheers later built his garage, was a fine old manor house, occupied by the Lewin family.

We now come to Hawarden Way, and on the corner, Mancot chapel, at the time of our walk plans had been laid for the construction of the new chapel, but of course the chapel then was the building that later became the church hall. Here let us divert a little, as we stroll to the area of another Mancot colliery of the past, this is the one where we see the Buckley tramway running through the woods. Near here we find Scotch Row (now the adjacent site of council houses) in that row lived two notorious characters, brothers Pinky and Ben. Now they were two very rough old men, of whom we youngsters were scared stiff, we certainly always gave them a wide berth! Nearby was Brown's farm, but Mr. Brown was very versatile, he ran a dairy farm and a very successful coal business, it was he who owned one of the first motor lorries in the village.

Let us now continue our *walk* down the other side of the horseshoe. I recall many of the families via the children who attended school with me, and on the right was Colin Pring (later a member of the Boy Scouts with me) then comes Audrey Lee, she was a quiet and intelligent girl who only spoke when absolutely necessary. Then came the two scallywags of my class, first of them was Len Jones, who we always referred to as 'Skippy' and the second, living next door, was Georgie Smith. Across the road, first a large house in its own grounds, this had been the residence of the manager of the munitions works during the war, next came the Bellis family. Their daughter Myfanwy, later married Bert Williams, son of the famous T.I. Williams of Deeside. The next plot, now occupied by a Mr and Mrs Lammond, stood a fine wooden building which housed the business of 'Beech the Barber'. Mr. Beech was a fine figure of a man, an ex WW1 Sgt. Major, he had a smart waxed moustache. His establishment was always spick and span and run along strict military lines; if you were in the queue for a short back and sides, when he shook his cloth and said, "next please" you jumped to attention, and reported to his chair smartly, or you were in dire trouble!

Down a little footpath to the left was the home of Ellis Eccles, who at that time had just started a Wolf Cub pack in the church hall. I later joined the Boy Scouts with him when he transferred to Sandycroft. Then, a little further, we crossed a small wooden bridge over a stream and came to the wooden bungalow occupied by the large, but very happy Bunnell family. Continuing down Hawarden Way, on the left were Bill and Tommy Edwards, and Gilbert Carter (Gib). The families of Airmen from RAF Sealand and my close friend Arthur Harrison occupied the row on the right. Arthur was not only a bosom school pal, but also a wartime comrade in the RAF, and eventually, best man at our wedding. Next to his house was Stokes' shop, and then of course that fine example to us all, Mr. John Evans, officer in the St. John's Ambulance Brigade. Back across in The Square, I remember the Gribble, Davies, McHugh and Reynolds families.

Let us now divert into Cross Ways, my own little neck of the woods. I have already mentioned the old fire station, now developed into Billy Hughes' grocery store, and Mr. Vyse, who ran a paper round but now we are confronted with what we always considered to be the village centre, "The Lawn". This was a large, enclosed, grassed playing area, where we children used to have a great time playing games. All of the houses surrounding it were elevated, all having half a dozen steps up to the front door, making it an ideal stadium. My outstanding memory of the lawn was the cricket matches the local lads held during summer evenings, which were thoroughly enjoyed by all the families perched on the doorsteps, there was no traffic of course at that time, what would be the chances of that today?

I turn back the clock now and recall the names of all those lads who took part. I wonder could they be Grandfathers of anyone living in the area today? The games were always organised by the Hooper boys, Robin and David, they were the sons of the estate manager who lived nearby, and they owned the Bat and Ball! Other names that I recall were, Dennis Ramshaw who was a good fast bowler, Cliff Talbot, Tommy Nock, Alan Martin, Ralph Rowlands, Ronny Peck, Cliff Meecock, Fred Evans, Frank Fennah, Raymond Trueman, & Eric Vyse. What fun those lads used to have, and I don't ever remember a broken window.

Another character that I associate with summer evenings on the lawn, was Ernie Massey. Ernie was a Happy go lucky person, he loved children and 'wouldn't hurt a fly', and he was a great athlete. He had represented Wales at soccer, and had been a renowned swimmer, but sadly, by the early 20's, poor Ernie was a slave to the demon drink.

Always on a Friday (payday) Ernie would suddenly appear among us kids, and quickly organise races on the lawn for the different groups. All the winners would be given Ernie's hard earned pennies.

He always used to finish his visit with a challenge, he would run backwards, but as he was always the fastest we could never catch him!! With that little finale, he would race away all smiles, the next stop Marcus's White Bear, to spend the rest of his wages. Another regular visitor to the village in those days was Lewis' ice cream cart; it came all the way from Chester. If it arrived when we were out playing Mrs Hooper would always treat us to a ½ penny cornet; that ice cream was out of this world!

It was only a short distance from the lawn to Mancot Lane, by Mrs Price's cottage, but here we had the assembly hall, which we used to call the church hall. Many travelling theatre groups performed there and every Saturday night it was a dance hall when all the locals danced to the strains of the Jim Davies dance band. Next was Peter Croft's butcher shop, a *butty* of his pork dripping was a treat. Right next-door was a little wooden fish and chip shop and supper bar run by Mr & Mrs Hughes, later taken over by Gib Carter and Amy. Opposite the fish and chip shop was a footpath leading to what we referred to as the backfield. This was an old recreation ground with swings etc. and was a relic of the first world war. In the 20's, it was very neglected and overgrown but a wonderful place to build camps, we used to have a great time there.

Continuing down Mancot Way we would pass the Davies' family home, Stan being another one of my schoolmates. Then it was the Bell's house; Mr Bell was a shunter at the Black Works. Next along was Roberts the Barber; his lads Glynne and Bill were also school pals. Mr Roberts could do an economy "short back and sides" in his kitchen for 1 penny, I was a regular visitor. Next to the barber's shop was the Evans', then Mrs Butler with the Pentre Chippy followed by Sam Griffith's family and then the Mountfords. On the left was the Fergusons, son Len being another school mate, then the Beech and

Cooper families. In the Cul-de-Sac were the families of Idris Pearsall, David Ellis and Ken Prestage.

In the Air Force houses lived Bob Ashcroft, who was in the Boy Scouts with me and across the road next to Alan Catherall's family, Mr Wild had a successful grocery business, which he conducted, from a wooden shed in his garden. On the corner of Hawarden Way, there was a long narrow row of low buildings, these were the estate offices which were later converted to a bungalow for the Harris family; later still they were demolished to make way for Ben Williams to construct half a dozen houses.

Across the road lived Joe Cone, a very enterprising man who would have a go at anything to make money. This ranged from a taxi service to the production of washing flakes and later a very successful printing works. As a youngster, I used to watch him printing in his garden, amongst other things Joe used to print a "freebie" leaflet for local distribution. Further down Hawarden Way was the Catherine Gladstone Maternity Home, where my wife Dot was to work during the war years.. Across the road again lived Mr Pryddyrch, the tenor and in the end house our very own village "bobby", the renowned Police Constable Baker; the very threat of this disciplinarian was enough to make all local kids "toe the line".

Finally, on the left, the old recreational club, which became the Conservative club and opposite, was Ellis' Dairy Farm. Mr Ellis used to deliver milk using a pony and trap and when he was on his rounds he could be heard from a long way off. The poor man had Parkinson's disease, then known as The Shakes and when measuring a pint of milk from his urn the noise was deafening, but he never did spill a drop!

To complete the walk we now go to Second Pentre where there was a row of shops on the other side of the main road. The right-hand side corner shop was Williams' Bakery and Post Office; the bakery was run by the son Emrys and the Post Office by his sister "Miss" Williams. She was a very haughty person, so much so that nobody dared ask her Christian name. Next to the bakery Mrs Pringle had her butcher's shop, she was my mate Arthur's grandmother and a widow who ran the shop with the help of her son-in-law Arthur Lever. Arthur was ex RAF and he later took over the business. Next to the butcher's shop was Mrs Darby's, her shop always smelled of paraffin, what she sold apart from that I can not remember but her son Harry, not much of a business man, used to sell firewood for his mum, from a handcart.

At the bottom of Rector's Lane, alongside the railway, was Nutona, a thriving business run by Mr Peck who lived in Hawarden Way, his son Ronny played cricket with us. This was a WW1 building in which he produced all kinds of nut delicacies using Brazil nuts. Outside his factory were mountains of nutshells and every Saturday morning he would allow us lads to go there with our handcarts to load up with shells to take home for burning. They provided excellent fuel and when mixed with coal certainly helped our parents with the fuel bill.

Earlier in this chapter I made reference to the motor vehicles in our village but failed to mention one of great importance to our lives in the early 1920's. This vehicle was our very first pioneering public service vehicle, the Red Warrior. A gentleman introduced this early bus to our roads just after the First World War; his name was Mr Crowther. He was a very astute businessman, well known and highly respected in Mancot. This early Ford twenty-seated bus had been painted red hence the name which was painted on the side. The little bus had twenty wooden seats with no upholstery! To us though it was a great innovation and a big step forward; a ride in it was a great adventure.

Mr Crowther was originally from Lancashire but had settled in Connah's Quay where he established an hourly bus service around Deeside. He also provided the occasional service to Chester, which I recall, cost the princely sum of four pence return. He also ran a school service at 08.30 each morning up to Hawarden costing a halfpenny. It was only in extremely bad weather that we used the service; normally we just walked there. However, I recall one particularly harsh frosty morning when we had the luxury of using Mr Crowther's bus and his son George was sitting up front with his dad. George was apparently learning to drive but was sitting on two sacks and carried a shovel! When we came to the clip near the cemetery we discovered the reason for this; the wheels started to slip! The bus was fitted with the latest pneumatic tyres but as there were very few motoring laws in those days, which meant that tyres could be used until they were bald. George got out of the bus and dug in front of the outer back wheel allowing him to place the sack there. As the wheel gripped and the bus moved forward onto the sack so George would put the second sack until the bus moved onto that. He then moved the first sack to the front of the wheel and the process was repeated until the bus reached the top of the hill.

Eventually another far-sighted businessman appeared on the scene, a Mr Crossland-Taylor and he introduced a bus called The Red Dragon. This operated an hourly service, on the half-hour before Mr Crowther's. This infuriated Mr Crowther and he fought tooth and nail to defeat the opposition. One idea that he had was to install a blue lamp on the top of his bus and use the slogan, "When out at night, look out for the blue light". Another ruse was to organise special outings and one particular trip was a Sunday school outing for our chapel to Rhyl. He crammed 30 people onto his 20-seated bus, which was against the law at that time as no standing passengers were allowed. However Mr Crowther sought to overcome that problem by devising a plan that whenever we saw a Bobby on point duty he would shout, "Everybody down" and all standing passengers would lie on the floor!

Once the danger of detection was over he would then shout instructions for us to stand up again. Using that method he got us to Rhyl and back *safely* and we all enjoyed a great day out.

By the early 1930's, Crossland-Taylor, having more financial clout, introduced a second Red Dragon expanding his service. Mr Crowther could no longer compete and so he sold out to Crossland-Taylor who then expanded further. Purchasing garages in Flint, Crossland-Taylor established the public transport company Crosville and this firm ruled the roost for many years. It was very ironic that George Crowther, son of the Mr Crowther, sought and obtained employment with Crosville as a driver! Mr Crowther senior used his hard earned cash to set up

Harold Donnell

a very successful fish and chip shop in Sandycroft; which just goes to show, you can't keep a good man down!

Hawarden Infants School 1924

Mr Crowthers bus

Jubilee bridge, Queensferry

Collecting tolls on the old Jubilee bridge, Queensferry

Chapter 2

All About Hawarden

Having concluded the Mancot *walk*, I think it appropriate to return up the hill to Hawarden to relive some of my early days at the school. I can still clearly picture the morning at the start of the term following summer holidays. A very smart tall gentleman was collecting a group of us children, who had reached the age for transfer to the "big" school. He was dressed in an immaculate tweed suit, highly polished brown shoes and sporting a very trim military style moustache. This gentleman was the well-respected Hawarden character and headmaster of Cannon Drew School, Major Maldwyn Davies. I am sure that we children must have felt some apprehension as, in line, we followed this very imposing figure through the churchyard and down the footpath. This footpath led to a gate in the boundary wall onto Gladstone Way and directly opposite the gateway to the playground of Cannon Drew School.

Five very formative years of my life were spent at this school and I feel that I can never repay my debt to the teachers at that time for their help in forming my character and instilling in me a constant desire, throughout a long life, to search for knowledge. This school, as you can gather from the Education Authority's choice of Head, was run on strict military lines, from the word go, everyone knew the rules and precisely how to toe the line! Major Davies had chosen his staff very carefully and I feel that he had got the balance just right.

Our introduction was indeed severe; we felt that we had entered the realm of a fire-breathing dragon in the form of Miss Mary Davies! That was the equivalent of being thrown in at the deep end, every moment of her presence was one of endeavour to please her. She constantly marched around the class, breathing *fire* down our necks, carrying a ruler with which she wrapped our knuckles for the slightest error. It was thanks to Miss Mary that I developed a good hand (handwriting). We had an inkwell on each desk and a scratchy pen on which you had to get the correct amount of ink; otherwise a large blot would result. She constantly preached to us, "Thin up, thick down and get the angle right". I received many a wrap on the knuckles, encouraging me to get it right.

Leaving the trauma of standard 1 and entering standard 2 was akin to coming indoors from a storm! Our teacher here was a very patient and quietly spoken, Miss Claudia Jones, a lovely lady who, by her gentle persuasive manner, made us all strive to do our best to please her. I can picture her now standing in front of the class, always beautifully turned out, with her hair in two buns, one over each ear, quite a fashionable style at that time.

In standard 3 we once again entered stormy waters, this time the domain of Mr Richard Iball. Dicky, as he became known, was only small but again immaculately turned out. He lived in the Buckley area and used to ride to school on a green Raleigh bicycle. He was a good teacher but his only downfall was a very short fuse and he used to vent his frustration on wayward pupils with a liberal use of his cane, which he did not spare at any time! I think I owe my love of gardening to Dicky and the school allotment, which is now the car park of the Masonic Hall. We lads spent many hours there with him cultivating a love of mother earth. However, my most lasting memory of Mr Iball is of his physical prowess.

Each morning we had an assembly parade and Dicky was always in charge of the boys' side, he would stand on the high steps by the entrance doors to inspect his *troops*. The small lads of standard 1 in the front line and in the back line at the top of the slope the big lads of standard 6. One morning I recall, following an incident in class the previous day, when one of the Price boys, Cyril, from Mancot Lane had been rather disruptive. To deal with this Dicky had administered the cane and given Cyril a good thrashing, which had drawn blood. Things were going as usual and to plan during the following morning's parade and just as Dicky was drawing us to attention, one of the big lads in standard 6 shouted, "Look out Dicky, here comes Mr Price"! Milden Wyatt, the boy in question, was quite a character; he later became a sergeant major in the Welsh Guards during WW2. As our master looked around we could detect a look of terror in his eyes as he saw Mr Price whose face was blue with rage.

Propping his bicycle up against the school railings, Mr Price rushed towards our disciplinarian, obviously intent on revenge. Amid a great deal of cheering from the assembled lads, Dicky rushed down the steps and at great speed he took to his heels, with Mr Price in pursuit. They completed two laps of the schoolyard and to this day I am not sure whether we were cheering for Dicky to escape or for Mr Price to catch him! Eventually, our super-fit master outran the older man and made good his escape up the school steps and into the school, locking the doors behind him. Dicky must have been breathlessly explaining his predicament to Maldwyn Davies because eventually this elegant military figure emerged and confronting Mr Price he spoke quietly but firmly to him. Mr Price agreed that he had made his point and mounting his bicycle he departed. We all noted that from that moment on, Dicky's enthusiasm for administering the cane seemed to have cooled off.

If we had considered standard 3 to be stormy waters we were in for a shock with our next move. In charge of standard 4 was the notorious Molly Bailey, this good lady had been hand picked by Maldwyn. Of immaculate appearance, clad in a tweed costume, wearing woollen golfing style stockings and highly polished brown shoes, her first comment when entering the classroom each morning was, "SILENCE! It's like bedlam in here". At first we kids did not understand what she meant by bedlam but believe me, we soon got to know that she was the one to sort it out. Miss Bailey ruled that class with a rod of iron and my lasting memory of her was one day when she dealt with Big Bill Roberts, son of Roberts the barber. Bill sat next to me in class and being so tall could easily look over my shoulder. This particular day Miss Bailey was busy marking our class work when she discovered that Bill's paper was word for word the same as mine. She dragged him out by his ear, although he towered above her, she proceeded to give him a good thumping, not with a stick but with her fists! After beating him to submission she made him sit at the back of the class on his own.

Our next move was to sail into the very calm waters of Miss Hopkins and standard 5. She was a very gentle lady, compared to Miss Bailey, and she hailed from Deeside. Miss Hopkins was cast in the Claudia Jones mould, no bullying, just gentle persuasion and I am sure that everybody did their best to please her. Our final move at the age of 12 was into standard 6, the domain of our illustrious headmaster, Major Maldwyn Davies. Although this was the move we had dreaded, we found him to be very strict but very fair and if you behaved yourself he treated you well. I remember that his favourite subject was Geography. He would spread large maps of the world on the board and easel and proudly point, with a very long cane, to all the parts of the world coloured pink, this was the British Empire! Mr Davies was one of the "old-school", I wonder what he would think of world affairs today?

Whilst at Cannon Drew School we were constantly told by our teachers of the many historical connections with the village of Hawarden and the surrounding areas. We were told about the famous people from the past, who were native of this amazing little village. Those seeds so carefully sewn have resulted in me pursuing the subject throughout my life.

It would be appropriate here to take a *stroll* through the village, which is barely half a mile in extent along the Ridgeway from the upper or the Western Cross, to the lower or Eastern Cross. These two crosses marked the village boundary. Unfortunately the Western Cross was removed during the late 19th century, at the time when the railway cutting was made, this was to make way for housing development. During the Industrial Revolution the village of Hawarden must have been a dusty, smoky place, as there were two iron works just outside each cross; Ratcliff's at the west and Rigby's at the east. Quite near the Western Cross is the mysterious Truman's Hill, and I believe that Willett got it right when he stated in his famous book, "History of Hawarden" that he believed this to be the burial mound of a Welsh prince who was slain in a battle here against the Norman, Henry II in 1157.

Just below our school was Deniol's Ash Manor House, which we used to pass every day on our way to and from school. Here, it was reputed, Saint Deniol landed in the 6th century, after having established a monastery at Bangor and planted his preaching staff, resolving to establish a Christian community in this beautiful spot.

Continuing along the Ridgeway, near to the cenotaph where Gladstone Way was constructed in the 19th century, preserved in a wall could be seen the original village pump; this was the only supply to the village for hundreds of years. Behind the wall is Saint Deniol's Library and Parish Church. The library is on the site of the original boys Grammar School, established in the 17th century where Richard Willett was headmaster for many years. The church, a Norman building, is on the site of the original Saint Deniol's church, a wattle and daub structure but the entire enclosure is said to date back to possibly the Stone Age.

This is an appropriate moment to tell the story of the Rood. It would appear that soon after the establishment of Saint Deniol's first church the lord of the manor occupied a residence near the present Deniol's Ash farm and that his lady, a very devout Christian, was in the daily habit of going to church to pray. In the naïve of that building a very crude and heavy wooden crucifix, or rood, had been erected but not very securely attached. It would appear that during one of her daily visits, when she was desperate to have her prayers answered, she flung her arms around the rood causing it to become detached. Both lady and cross fell to the ground; the heavy cross fell on top of the lady killing her instantly.

The heartbroken lord called upon a jury of local men to pronounce on this terrible event and the jury eventually agreed that the rood was guilty of murder. They could not decide what form the punishment should take but one member suggested that the rood should be beheaded. This was greeted with horror, then one bright young man, "Leech" of Mancot, proposed that they carry the rood in procession, down to the riverbank and at high tide they should cast it into the water. So they all agreed to this solution where the rood would be swept out to sea and all their troubles would go with it. Of course, on the day concerned, what the locals had not considered was that the high tide of those days was an incoming tide and so the rood, instead of being swept out to sea was carried up river. Eventually it came to rest on a sandbank in the old harbour at Chester, just below the city walls.

The story by this time became common knowledge to the citizens of Chester and when they found the rood they indignantly erected it on the site. They attached a plaque to it, which read, "The Jews the Lord did crucify, but the Hawardeners He did drown". Today can be seen a small stone plinth on that spot in the centre of the Roodee racecourse explaining the origin of its name.

Returning to The Ridgeway walk, we now make our way up Gladstone Way and just below Cannon Drew School could be seen a small stone-built, thatched cottage. This was the famous Polly Irmstone's abode where a true "Cottage Industry" thrived for many years as the most delicious toffee was produced here. During the 20's, Polly's daughter, Mrs Durham carried on the business, still using the same recipe and skills, she produced the same "melt in the mouth" toffee, a bargain at 1/2d for four large squares. Just above Cannon Drew was another famous stone building, which was then, as now the Masonic Hall. Previously it had been the National Boy's School, constructed in the days when it was not deemed appropriate to educate young girls, the majority ending up "in service".

Again now on The Ridgeway, near to the cenotaph and a few yards to the east is where Mr Dann's chemist shop stands, previously this had been another small, stone, thatched cottage. This old cottage had been the home of Mrs Kidd, grandmother to Emma Lyons, the future Lady Hamilton; it was in that humble abode that the illustrious lady had spent her childhood. Emma was born in Ness, on the Wirral, in 1765. Her father was the village blacksmith but died when she was a babe in arms and so it was that her mother returned to her native Hawarden. Mrs Kidd, a widow, who brought up the child, must have been a tough character as she ran the family haulage business single-handed. This business used Shire horses and large wagons and the stables and stores were behind the cottage in what was later to be known as Rickett's yard.

From an early age Emma had a good voice, you could imagine her taking part in services at St Deniol's church; she also showed theatrical promise. In her early teens she obtained employment, in service for Dr Thomas just across the road, the property was just on the corner where the HSBC Bank now stands. It seems that during her employment she developed a skin complaint and Dr Thomas recommended that she have a holiday at Parkgate, on the Wirral, to try the "novel idea" of sea bathing as a cure.

Across Rectory Drive, in a large house called Kentagern, lived the Boydell family, who for many years and generations were agents for the Glyn estate. One of the sons, John, became a famous figure; he was probably a contemporary of Emma. John had an artistic flare and as a young boy was intrigued by the work of an engraver who came to make a copper plate of Hawarden castle. He was so impressed that as a teenager, he walked all the way to London to seek out the engraver and as a result was apprenticed by him. After some years he was so talented that he took over the control of the company and eventually he became the Lord Mayor of London.

It was probably on account of this connection that Emma eventually went to London to further her ambition to become an actress. This beautiful girl succeeded and moved into high society living and finally married Lord Hamilton who was then the Ambassador to Naples. It was at that location that Emma first met Admiral Nelson when his fleet put in there for refit following the battle of the Nile. It was there that he had defeated Napoleon's French fleet and had become a national hero; the rest of the story is history!

At the end of Rector's Lane is the rectory, a very old building steeped in history but more recently it was home to the young men of the Knutsford Test School. This had been the brainchild of Reverend "Tubby" Clayton, the founder of TOCH, and was for the training of young men for the Christian ministry. These were men who had pledged their lives to the church following their dreadful experienced in World War 1. Many hundreds of ministers were trained here in the 20's and 30's.

Back onto The Ridgeway could be seen the Glyn Arms, a famous staging inn in the days of stage coach travel when Hawarden was on the Chester to Holyhead route. Directly opposite is the very imposing main entrance to Hawarden Castle. In the 19th century it was a regular sight here on Sunday mornings, when the "old man" was at home, to see Mr & Mrs Gladstone, together with their servants, proceeding to morning service at St Deniol's parish church. Of course, in the middle of the road junction today is the fountain erected by the parishioners in memory of Mr & Mrs Gladstone. In the 20's the fountain was still functioning and on hot summer days we often used to pause there for a drink of the beautiful cold water.

Beyond the grand entrance was Hawarden Castle, which was not normally accessible to the general public. The original, constructed soon after the Norman Conquest, was an earthen Mote and Bailey, granted by William to the Earl of Chester. A stone structure was later built and in the 13th century this was captured by Dafydd ap Griffith, an action which sparked Edward I to declare outright war on the Welsh. By the 15th century the lordship was granted to the Stanleys (Earl of Derby), a position they held until the conclusion of the civil war in the mid 17th century.

During the war Lord Stanley declared for the Royalists and held the castle for the King. With the final parliamentary victory Lord Stanley was sent to London to be tried with Charles the first and it was there that he was executed as a traitor. The lordship was then presented to John Glynn of Caernarfon who had been a general in Cromwell's army. With the collapse of Cromwell's government and the restoration of the monarchy, the King knighted John Glynn for his help in the restoration!! So within a short time one Hawarden ruler lost his head for supporting the king and another received a knighthood for the same.

By the 18th century the old castle was untenable and eventually the famous architect, Joseph Turner, a resident of the village, built the new castle. Eventually the male line of the Glynn family ended and W E Gladstone married the only daughter, Catherine and so inherited the lordship. It must be noted that throughout his long term as prime minister the famous W E Gladstone did not hit it off with Queen Victoria. She did not like the way he addressed her and so to the end of his days he remained plain Mr W E Gladstone. It was the Glynn family who enclosed Hawarden Park with a boundary wall and constructed the water mill in the popular Mill Woods. Unfortunately little remains today of the old mill but the site is still worth a nostalgic visit.

Continuing along what was the Ridgeway but now known as Glynn Way, a row of ancient stone cottages can be seen on the right. The last cottage is now an antique shop but in the early 19th century it was a saddler's shop where W Bell-Jones served his apprenticeship with his father. He later opened the first post office in the village, which was directly across the road from the saddlers. It was W Bell-Jones who sent the message out to the nation when Mr Gladstone passed away and subsequently, he played a major role in village life.

Next we pass the old council offices and come to Cross Tree Lane where on the junction can be seen the old tree planted in the 17th century marking the spot of the eastern cross. To the rear can be seen the House of Correction, a lock-up designed by Joseph Turner, where anyone causing trouble in the village could be detained overnight. The police constable who lived nearby would control this together with the use of the stocks and whipping post which existed back then; hard old days! As we continue we reach the imposing building known as The Elms, the previous home of Joseph Turner who was responsible for some of the early restoration work on the Chester City Walls and Bridge Gate in particular. He also supervised the redesign and building of Mold Parish Church and the magnificent, original, Ruthin Gaol was also his work.

Finally, on our left is the Memorial Institute, which housed one of the first lending libraries in the country, this was started with a collection presented to W E Gladstone by Isaac Pitman. We leave the village with the ancient smithy on our right and drop down a steep hill where the road was diverted to skirt the high wall, part of the Glynn's "enclosure".

The Reverend Cannon Drew

Sister Glenys and me

Cannon Drew School 1928.

WW1 Cannon in Hawarden recreation ground, 1920's

Hawarden Village

Hawarden village 1920's

Monument in the centre of Hawarden village

Knutsford Test School

St Deniol's Library

Hawarden Castle

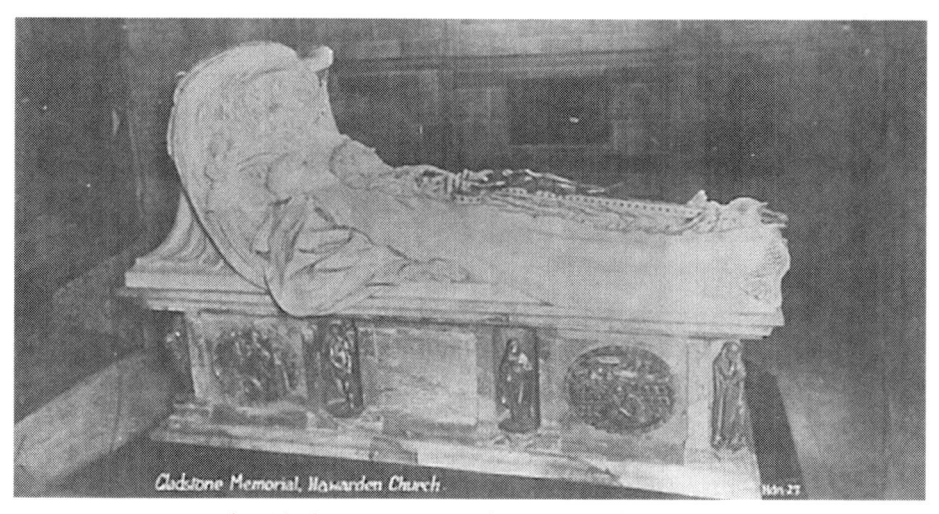

The Gladstone Memorial in Hawarden church

Chapter 3

Be Prepared for an Adventure Afloat

I was introduced to the Boy Scout movement in 1930, at the tender age of 10 years. I am proud of the fact that I remained an active member of that great movement into my teens and up to the advent of the Second World War. It was then that I found my Boy Scout training of immense value. My involvement in scouting was largely due to the perseverance of my bosom school buddy Arthur Harrison. From its inception Arthur had been a member of the Mancot Wolf Cub Pack, which had been formed in 1928 by our local stalwart Ellis Eccles. Meetings were held in the Mancot Church Hall and Arthur was constantly urging me to join up. I must digress for a moment to add that Arthur and I remained firm friends for many years; we both subsequently joined the RAF and served in the Middle East together. Following the hostilities of the war, Arthur was best man at Dot and my wedding in Mancot Chapel.

Returning to the scouting saga, Ellis Eccles had learned his Scouting in Deeside with Lieutenant / Commander Marriot, who had formed a Scout Troop in Connah's Quay. Marriot was an ex-naval officer who had been an acquaintance of Baden Powell during the Boar War, and after that conflict had worked with "BP" in founding the Scout

Movement. In the mid 1920's Marriot had taken his troop to attend the World Jamboree, held at Arrow Park in Birkenhead and there he introduced his boys to the great man himself. Ellis had been so fired up by that wonderful experience that he decided to form his own local Scout Group and so the 1st Mancot Wolf Cub Pack was born.

In 1930 Ellis was asked by the Rev. Hardcastle, the vicar of St. Frances Church in Sandycroft, if he would like to form a Boy Scout Troop. With this came the offer of free headquarters in the then redundant Manse at the village school. So Ellis moved in and the 1st Sandycroft (St. Frances) Boy Scout Troop came into being. It was at this time that we were in Miss Molly Bailey's class at the cannon Drew School in Hawarden, and one morning Arthur came to our school full of excitement. The latest news was that "Elli" (the name for Ellis affectionately given by the local boys) was organizing a camping holiday with a difference for the Troop; they were going to have two weeks on a barge on the Shropshire Union Canal. Ellis was a cavalier type of a lad and rallied all the boys to his idea; this even included the Rev. Hardcastle, who expressed his desire to accompany the troop on their "Great Adventure". When Arthur described the proposal to me in great detail, I too was so fired up and could not get down to Sandycroft with him quick enough to join up. However, I discovered that the initial requirement to join the Boy Scouts was that the applicant had to be 11 years old. Most boys in the Cub Pack had already reached that age, but I was only 10 years old; so I presented myself for enrolment with some apprehension.

On confronting Ellis I confessed my age, but stressing how keen I was to go on the canal with them. I was delighted when he said "Come on lad, you can join us", he was an expert at bending the rules. So very quickly I was drafted into the Badger Patrol, the Patrol Leader was Colin Pring of Mancot, and the Second my good friend Arthur. The first thing to do was to learn the Scout Promise: "On my honour, I promise that I will do my best, to do my duty to God and the King, to help other people at all times and to obey the Scout Law". When finally I could repeat these words by heart, I was enrolled into the troop. At our regular meetings we all worked hard at Scout Craft, learning all we could about good camping techniques, how to light fires without matches, the secrets of trekking, rope knot work and splicing, and signaling which included Morse Code and Semaphore. What I found most difficult of all was the learning of the Scout Law, which was based on the Ten Commandments. However, all of the time, excitement was building up as we all looked forward to "The Great Adventure Afloat".

My Mum and Dad were equally enthusiastic and were saving up to pay for my very first adventure holiday away from home. The going rate for a camp with our troop in 1930 was five shillings a week (25 pence in today's money), so our fortnight's adventure was going to cost ten shillings (50 pence). To put that in perspective my father's wage to support a family of six was just two pounds and ten shillings (£2.50), so that ten shillings was one fifth of his weekly earnings! Eventually however, by much thrift and sacrifice, they managed to come up with the required amount and looking back on it today, I suppose that holiday could be described as the ultimate economy cruise.

My first encounter with the Canal was a visit one weekend to the Tower Warf in Chester. There was of course no bus service in those days, so the only way of getting there was by "Shanks' Pony". The whole troop assembled and we set out early Saturday morning, to make our way via Garden City and Sealand Road. Some of the lads possessed pushbikes so we all took turns having a ride on the crossbar and of course everyone walked at "Scout Pace", which was walk twenty, run twenty. We must have been a tough little bunch, because in no time we arrived in Chester. The object of our visit was to select the narrow boat for our trip. Ellis had got the idea for the holiday from a contact of his on the LNER railway, where he worked as a trainee signalman at Liverpool Road Station, Chester. The canals were owned at that time by the railways and Ellis' contact had assured him that there were dozens of abandoned barges on the wharf, from which we could take our pick.

We were not prepared for the scene that was to confront us; on arrival it was one of sheer dereliction and decay. There were dozens of barges moored there, but all were rotting hulks, that had been abandoned thirty or forty year ago. They were all full of water, and resting on the bottom. As we hopped from one to the other, I must admit that we also began to get that sinking feeling. The man we had to contact for hiring a barge at the former boat-building yard was at that time attempting to clear the wharf by breaking up the old barges. Alongside the towpath he had a timber yard where he was reclaiming planking and had firewood for sale. However all was not lost as suddenly a cry went up from Jim Billingsley, one of our lads from the Pentre, "Here's a good one," he cried with delight. Sure enough as we all dashed over she was indeed a "good one". Jim had found a long abandoned "Shropshire Fly". The paintwork on her cabin was faded and flaking, but her name was quite discernable, "COMBERMERE". The barge family who had last sailed her had left all of the tarpaulin sheets in place over the hold, so keeping out the weather. Her timbers all seemed in sound condition and she was well and truly afloat.

Hopping eagerly aboard we soon discovered that her last cargo had been a load of coal, probably delivered to Black Diamond Street. This must have been a desperate and degrading load, for a Shropshire Fly, in their hey day had been the Aristocrats of the Waterways. Ellis and Hardy (our nickname for the Rev. Hardcastle) quickly decided that was our choice and did a deal with the boat yard owner come scrap dealer. The deal was struck to hire the barge for two weeks, for the princely sum of one pound and ten shillings. They also negotiated with another man local man who owned the canal side stables, to supply a horse to tow the barge.

As we eagerly hauled the Combermere alongside the towpath for tidying up, our spirits were high. For the next few weeks it was a case of "all hands on deck". The whole troop worked hard to get our dear old narrow boat in good order, all "Ship Shape and Bristol Fashion". The fortunate ones who possessed pushbikes, Ellis and some of the senior scouts, did most of the restoration work, being able to get to Chester fairly easily in the evenings. At the weekend we younger scouts would make our usual trek into Chester and *chip in*. The dust and grime from years of neglect were swept away and the hold where we would sleep was scrubbed down.

The tiny cabin was made spotless, brasses were cleaned and the coal fired range given a lick of black lead. Even the smaller forward locker (which had served as children's sleeping quarters) was cleared out, and the remains of the last cargo were shoveled into sacks for use on the range. What a sight she was, when the ornate paintwork was renovated and touched up. Contemplating the name we all began to wonder if she was named after the famous hero of the British Empire, who proudly rides his Bronze Horse at the entrance to the Chester Castle, if so what a pedigree!

Then finally, at the beginning of the school holidays in August 1930, the great day arrived. Ellis, Hardy and two of the older lads had set out on that Friday evening to sleep onboard and prepare things for us boys. The rest of the troop left Mancot early Saturday morning, kit bags over our shoulders, and began our trek to Chester. I recall that my dad could not afford a proper kit bag, so my mum made me one out of an old pillowcase, into which I put all items required for the holiday; these included:

- A change of clothes
- 2 blankets
- A towel
- A bar of lifebuoy soap.
- Tooth brush and tooth paste.
- Knife, fork, spoon, plate and mug
- Brush and Comb.

So with these possessions slung over my shoulder I proudly set off with the other boys, singing Scouting songs as we marched along. The miles simply flew by, and we arrived at Tower Wharf by late afternoon. What a reception we had on our arrival, Ellis, Hardy and the older scouts had dressed up as pirates. They had neckerchiefs knotted around their heads in "Long John Silver" fashion and the only thing missing was a "Jolly Roger" flying from the stern. "Welcome aboard me hearties" cried Ellis, and as we all wearily occupied our allotted sleeping space in the hold, giant jam butties and mugs of cocoa were dished out, what a great start to our adventure!

How well I remember that first night aboard, making up our beds in that hold, bathed by the light from hurricane lamps, we were then plied with more jam butties and cocoa. The Rev. Hardy told us stories of why the Romans had chosen Chester to build their Great Fortress and then how pioneers had constructed their canals in the 18th and 19th centuries. This opened up the country for the industrial revolution. Hardy was a great storyteller and I suppose you could describe these as the ultimate bedtime stories. He filled our young minds with so much enthusiasm for the forthcoming trip so that, on our first night aboard, we all slept very soundly.

We woke up at the crack of dawn, and of course the first order of the day was a hearty breakfast for twenty hungry lads. That first catering attempt resulted in a great deal of amusement and finally hearty peals of laughter all around. Our two leaders had agreed that Ellis would be Skipper and Hardy would be First Mate, and therefore had allocated themselves the tiny cabin, with its cozy bunk beds. The cooking range had a liberal supply of coal, they intended to do all the cooking and dish it out to us boys as we lined up in the hold. The scheme, however, very quickly backfired. They found that there was a blockage in the flue, because as soon as the range was stoked up, the cabin became full of thick black smoke. The sight of our two gallant officers, with blackened faces, staggering out of the cabin, eyes streaming, and gasping for air raised howls of laughter, nobody envied them their *first class* accommodation! Immediately we realized that the onboard cooking facilities were totally inadequate to feed the troop. Therefore we would have to resort to the traditional campfire. This was quickly carried out using the good scout practice we had been taught, which included clearing all evidence of the fire afterwards, and leaving the towpath as we found it. This was so successful that we repeated it throughout the trip.

Breakfast over and the gear stowed, the next stage was the arrival of our horsepower, and sure enough, as promised the old man appeared with a beautiful stallion. He expertly coupled the towrope to Combermere and very quickly, we were whisked across the wharf, to the Northgate Staircase of canal locks. We lads gazed in wonder at this great feat of engineering, simply by transferring water from one chamber to another, boats could be raised through a series of locks, something like 50 feet from the basin to the higher canal level.

Now our cruise really got underway, our mighty steed was a beauty and Combermere proved to be an excellent vessel. To our amazement there appeared high cliffs on either side of the canal, from where we could hear the beats from the horse's hooves, echoing loudly. It was at this point that Hardy began to give us a running commentary. The canal builders, he explained, had used the Roman moat to skirt the city and the cliffs we saw were in fact the sides of the quarry that they had excavated to build the fortress. The resulting moat had provided the defense for the Northern Boundary. As we progressed, Hardy pointed out the Northgate Bridge, high above us, which had originally been a drawbridge, and the high city walls. In our creative imaginations we expected at any moment to see a Roman guard gazing down to challenge us.

At the North Eastern corner of the City Walls, he pointed out King Charles Tower. It was here that during a visit to Chester, the King had observed his army defeated at the Battle of Rowton Moor, a decisive battle during the Civil War. The first test of Ellis' skill at the tiller came when we encountered Cowlane Bridge; it was very narrow, only allowing a few inches of leeway, for a narrow boat. Our Shropshire Fly, with it's strong horse, was probably exceeding the speed limit of 3 MPH, so Ellis gave the timbers a hefty whack on the abutment, much to the disgust of the old bargee, who grunted his disapproval. During our trip however, we all had a go on the tiller and became quite experts at negotiating these narrow bridges.

Leaving the city, the canal continued to rise at the locks near Long Lane, after which we crossed a small aqueduct over the Chester to Crew railway line. Finally we arrived at a tidy looking 19th century warehouse near Christleton. We passed by several large houses with high hedges and gardens sweeping down to waters edge. This area was later to become "Dean's Marina" and I would like to think that Mr. Dean peeped over his high hedge and thought, "now that's a good idea". As we journeyed on, to our right was pointed out Rowton Moor, the scene of the Civil War battle.

Very soon, upon reaching open countryside, it was decided that it was time to stop for dinner. The towpath campfire was setup and the potatoes and fresh vegetables had been obtained from a canal side farm were prepared. In no time the dixies were merrily boiling to provide a well deserved midday meal. The canals were little used at that time, and in places, almost choked up with weeds, but the water was clear and as fresh as a mountain stream, so we simply threw buckets overboard to collect our cooking and drinking water. On discovering that the water was quite shallow, with shouts of glee we all jumped in for a splash around. We noted however, that on this first exciting day of our adventure, the old bargee had not made any conversation and kept himself to himself. He did not seem to appreciate the sense of thrill and adventure we boys were enjoying. Maybe he felt that we cheeky youngsters were intruding into a world in which we were not wanted.

With the combination of a powerful horse and a good fast narrow boat our progress on the first day was astonishing; by the late afternoon we were approaching Beeston. Everyone felt confident regarding our proposed round trip to Whichurch. Arriving at Beeston we moored up near the famous "Iron Rock" and set up our usual towpath campfire. We were all chatting happily as we squatted around preparing the evening meal when the equivalent of a bombshell was dropped. The old bargee came over and declared, **"Well, this is as far as I go"**. Everyone looked up at him in disbelief, what on earth was he talking about? Our adventure had only just begun! All evening Ellis and Hardy tried reasoning with him, but to no avail, his mind was made up. So it was with heavy hearts that we bedded down for the night.

Early next morning we were left in no doubt at all, that the old man packed his few belongings, mounted his trusty steed and disappeared down the towpath on his way back to Chester. I have subsequently wondered, could we really blame him, as during the first days some of the lads had been laughing and referring to themselves as "Water Gipsies". Had he looked upon this as an insult and been offended?

For whatever reason he and his horse had deserted us. A feeling of utter despair clouded over us at breakfast, was this to be the end of our trip? Would we spend the rest of the holiday at Beeston? However, Ellis was not a man to let a little upset like this spoil his plans. As we all sat there, full of doom and gloom, he suddenly shouted, "Well, me hearties, are we just going to stop here or are we going to pull the barge ourselves?"

The proposal that the leaders had come up with was, that Ellis would lead the Badger Patrol, and Hardy would lead the Bulldogs. Between us we would "bow haul" Combermere for the rest of the holiday. Everyone greeted the wonderful plan with so much enthusiasm that we all let out a mighty cheer. The wise Hardy though, despite smiling with the rest of us, raised his arms to calm us down, pointed up to the ruined castle on the hill top he said "steady on boys, too much noise may awaken the ghosts slumbering up there." We didn't quite know what he was indicating, but as he was always quietly reading his history books in the tiny cabin, we assumed he was preparing another one of his little stories. Hardy had already explained to us the reason for the unusual iron lock and that the original stone lock had collapsed, flooding the area. However, Telford had designed this huge iron box, which has stood the test of time, being used successfully today. That evening we all settled down on our bedrolls, anticipating the ghost story, which we were sure Hardy had been carefully preparing.

I would like to add here, that I am grateful to the staff of the Beeston Castle visitor's centre, for refreshing my memory on the story, which went something like this:

"Boys, as we gaze up at Beeston Castle, on its lofty crag and study its very long and chequered history. We cannot but imagine that many troubled souls must be slumbering on that quiet hillside."

A Bit of History on Beeston Castle

The castle stands at the end of a chain of hills extending from southern Cheshire. The high ridge is some 500 feet above the Cheshire Plain. In days gone by, whoever occupied this spot had a great advantage. During the Bronze Age, it was no doubt a settlement or hill fort and from where there is a stunning view of the Plain. From the Penines in the East to the Welsh Mountains in the West, any enemy activity could be spotted quite easily. There is no mention of it during the Roman period, when it was probably ruthlessly destroyed; there is evidence though of a Roman Road nearby. The building of the castle on that location began following the Norman Conquest when Ranulf, the Earl of Chester, in the 12th century, chose the spot for his castle. Having returned from the Crusades, he had learned a lot about castle building whilst in Syria and the Holy Land, and this knowledge he put to good use at Beeston.

In the 13th century Prince Edward, later to become King Edward I, visited the castle. It was to be used by him as a base for his war against North Wales. Much later, during the 14th century, King Richard II stayed there, prior to setting sail from Chester, to quell a rebellion in Ireland. On his return Richard was betrayed at Conway and imprisoned at Flint Castle by Lord Bolingbroke, whom subsequently had the King executed and had himself crowned Henry IV.

There is belief that King Richard buried some of his treasure in the deep well of the Inner Bailey at Beeston. By the 17th century however, the castle had fallen into disrepair and at the commencement of the Civil War, the Parliamentarians, whose headquarters were at nearby Nantwich, quickly seized and renovated it.

As a Castle in those days, it was considered impregnable; the command was given to a local Gentleman, Thomas Steele. He was a good administrator, but no soldier, along with his rank of Captain and a garrison of 60 men at Beeston, Parliament felt very secure indeed. However at this time, November 1643, the Royalist stronghold at Chester had been reinforced with troops from Ireland, who had arrived via the river Dee,. In this army was a certain Captain Thomas Sandford, who was a farsighted man, with very different views on waging war. Accessing the situation, he said to the powers that be, "give me eight good men of my choosing and I will give you Beeston Castle".

Sandford was probably the pioneer of what was to become the Commandos and Special Service Units in our Modern Army. In mid December 1643, he set out from Chester with his specially selected team. At his request, they had all been provided with the latest firearms (Fire locks) and all had coils of rope and grappling irons, slung over their shoulders. With blackened faces, they traveled only at night, lying concealed during the daylight hour avoiding detection. After several days of this stealthy approach they finally arrived at the foot of the steep Western cliff face. His timing was precise, Steele and his Garrison probably with the help of lots of home brew, had been celebrating the Advent of Christmas. Attacking at this time was contrary to the rules of chivalry, but in the early hours of the morning, with a little help from their climbing gear, they scaled the cliff and gained entry over the Castle walls.

The sudden appearance of these fierce looking warriors, with their modern weaponry, so terrified the garrison that they immediately surrendered the castle and its supplies. As was the rule of engagement in those days, Steele and his men were allowed to march out of the castle. With banners flying and Drums beating, the Parliament army made their way to Nantwich. However when the garrison arrived in Nantwich, Brereton, the General in charge of the northern army and his commanders showed their fury at the loss of Beeston. With this, Steele and his men were ridiculed as cowards and traitors. Following a Court Marshall, poor Steele faced execution. For their part on acquiring the Castle, the Royalists appointed a military man, Captain Vallett, as Governor, and so for the next two years it was held very securely indeed.

Later the tide of war finally flowed the other way, when the garrison lost contact with Chester, following the Battle of Rowton Moor, when the castle again came under siege by Parliament. Vallett and his men, who by this time were starving, were in their turn allowed to surrender and march out to an uncertain future. The Castle was again left to decay, as the Roundheads advanced on Chester. Hardy concluded, "These, then Boys, are just a few of the tormented souls whose ghosts must haunt that quiet and mysterious hill and who I think we should leave in peace". Needless to say, none of us boys needed rocking to sleep that night, having listened to such an enthralling yarn. The next morning, the third day of our holiday, we were all up at the crack of dawn and raring to go *bow hauling* once again.

As we traversed the locks, the lock keeper came out of his cottage to enquire on our progress. He must have taken pity on us, because, addressing Ellis he said, "I think I know someone with a horse who will tow you". Being full of youthful enthusiasm Ellis shouted back, "Don't bother, we will be alright". By bending our backs on the towrope we soon began to make good progress. The boat seemed quite light and easy to tow and the agreement was that each patrol did a half hour spell. We quickly discovered that, by changing over while keeping the boat in motion, we could keep a brisk pace. With our regular meal stops we found that in our first day of bow hauling, we had covered quite a few miles, with which we were all very pleased. However, after further discussion, as we were farther away from Whitchurch than we had anticipated, it was decided that we would just go as far as possible in the first week and then use the second week for the return journey.

The next morning, being our fourth day, was just to be a repeat of the previous day. We got up and away and a few miles later, at midday we hove to. Then we settled down by our campfire for a welcome dinner, peace however was soon disturbed by a lot of shouting from farther down the towpath. Upon investigation, it was revealed that an old man was approaching, leading a horse! The coarse language he used as he shouted at us did not come from the English dictionary; the air was blue with expletives and in embarrassment, the Rev. Hardcastle retreated to the safety of his cabin! It transpired that, for two days the old man had been unable to catch up with us, we all found this to be highly amusing and started laughing. Ellis seeing the old man in such a rage, showed some tact, and realizing also that the poor old man was probably starving, he walked down the towpath to meet him and shook his hand. He said, "Welcome friend, have you had your dinner?" He was then given a plate heaped with boiled potatoes, vegetables and half a tin of corned beef, all topped with a large chunk of butter. The transformation was magic, the face that was clouded with anger, suddenly beamed, from that moment the old man was our best friend. Between mouthfuls of food, he told us that his name was Joe, and he was a friend of the Beeston lock keeper! Joe had been born on a narrow boat and with his family had spent all his life "on the Cut". Now sadly, he was out of work and destitute, but he said he was prepared to tow our barge as long as we wanted; he knew a good billet when he saw one.

On preparing to move on with our new horsepower, we soon found out that Joe's poor horse was lame and unable to cope. He explained that his horse had been out in the field throughout the winter, was not shod and had grown enlarged hooves, which had become infected. We therefore decided to continue bow hauling, and let Joe lead his horse behind us, in the hope we could find someone to tend to his needs. Now we knew the reason they had been unable to catch up with us! Thankfully on arrival at Bunbury Staircase Locks, we found a canal side stables and a Blacksmith who was still in business. This good man promised that the next morning he would attend to poor old Dobbin. The next morning Ellis and Hardy agreed to front the bill, and we boys were a very attentive audience. The infected hooves were trimmed, with at least two or three inches taken off, the blacksmith then expertly treated the infection before giving our horse four new shoes.

As a result of this treatment the transformation was unbelievable, the old horse stamped up and down the towpath, as if to express his joy. When coupled to the barge, we could not hold him back, as well as towing the boat at great speed he let us have rides on his back, we took turns of course. Joe proved to be a wonderful traveling companion, he slept in the hold with us boys, and we loaned him some blankets. However at night he simply curled up on the deck, never bothering to remove his clothes. He was a hive of information, taking over from Hardy as the chief storyteller. We just could not contain him as he yarned on about his life on the canal and the wonders of the waterways. The reason for the canal locks and how they worked was explained, as was the Incline Planes, which Joe's family had used. These great feats of engineering consisted of sets of huge rollers, set on an incline between canals and rivers of differing levels. The traditional narrow boats were flat bottomed, sturdily built vessels to facilitate being hauled up and down these ramps by huge steam engines.

Our Shropshire Fly was not designed for this, having a rounded hull to allow for greater speeds. They were the aristocrats of the waterways, designed to carry more valuable cargo in an express service, between the industrial Midlands and the river Mersey at Ellesmere Port. We listened in suspense as we were told of long dark tunnels, drilled into the hills, which had no towpaths. There in total darkness, the entire barge family, men, women and children, would *leg it* on the tunnel sides to propel the boat. The horse would be taken over the top of the hill to meet them at the other side of the tunnel. Another story was of the great aqueduct over the river Dee Valley at Trevor, there the horse had to be blind folded to save it from panicking whilst crossing.

As the stories poured out Ellis decided to make our holiday a more leisurely affair, "Lets take it easy" he said, "and enjoy the old man's company". Whitchurch had been given up as our destination, in favour of Nantwich, and while passing Hurleston, Joe pointed out the fantastic series of 14 locks, by which boats could be taken up the hillside. This would allow us to join the Llangollen and Whitchurch canals. All this was the work of Thomas Telford, who had also constructed the Horse Shoe Falls, built to extract four million gallons of water a day from the river Dee, to feed the canal system.

We spent some considerable time at Barbridge and there we viewed the Middlewich Arm, another Telford undertaking. This is now a prosperous marina but in 1930, it was like Tower Wharf, derelict and forgotten, with rotting narrow boats moored there. Among these sad looking vessels Joe spotted a sturdy 25-foot boat, with reinforced iron bows. This he informed us was an Ice Breaker, a high iron rail ran down the centre of the vessel. By grabbing the rail, and standing on either side the bargees could rock the vessel, thus breaking the ice. In those days it was vital, he said, that barge families delivered their cargo on time; being frozen in during harsh weather could prove costly. So under Joe's guidance, we all eagerly hopped on board the icebreaker and spent a happy half hour joyfully "rocking the boat".

Looking like the scene of 77 years ago, near the Barbridge Hotel, with its modern Canal side Restaurant, stood a small white washed cottage; this had served, among other things as a general store. We then noticed that Joe was having an earnest conversation with Ellis and as we drew alongside he leaped ashore, his clogs beat a rapid tattoo on the steps as he dashed down to the shop. On returning aboard his face was a picture, Ellis had given him a shilling, to treat himself to a tin of Players Twist tobacco. Joe was like a dog with two tails, the rest of the holiday, he spent lovingly cutting thin slices of tobacco with his razor sharp penknife which he then rolled in his dirty hands, to fill his pipe; he was indeed a very contented man.

His old horse was happy as his master as Ellis had acquired a bag of oats and a bail of hay, which we had stowed in the forward locker. Each night Dobbin would have a good feed and settle down for a good nights sleep alongside the moored boat, without his poor *feet* killing him! They were now a happy team, a far cry from the bedraggled couple who had angrily managed to catch up with us a couple of day earlier. Eventually we approached what we had decided was the limit of our journey, Nantwich and after listening to Hardy's stories this place was very significant to us. We had traveled the full extent of the battle zone, from Royalist Chester to Parliamentary Nantwich. Our journey had been made easy though thanks to the canal builders of the 18th century, who had linked these two towns of commerce. The canal made it possible for large lighters, of some 14 feet beam, to trade between Nantwich and the newly cut River Dee channel, so opening up the world market to Cheshire's extensive agricultural produce. However, when we entered the Nantwich Warf, we were totally shocked by the scene of utter decay and neglect that confronted us. Tall, disused, warehouses surrounded the basin, with rotting doors swinging dejectedly from gaping holes, which had once been boarding bays. Joe pointed out to us Holland's warehouse from which the famous Cheshire Cheese had once been exported.

Despite the magnificent engineering and hard work that had gone into their construction, the canals had only enjoyed a very brief commercial life of some seventy or eighty years. By the mid 19th century along came Stephenson, with his rocket and the bargees found it impossible to compete with the ever-expanding railway system. The final attempt to compete came in the form of the express Shropshire Fly, but it was all in vain. Eventually the wealthy railways won and made a takeover bid, buying out the canal companies and thus leaving the waterways to decay. Having listened to so many of Joe's stories, we viewed that scene with sadness and now felt that we could understand the bitter attitude displayed by the few boat people we had encountered. They had been deprived of their way of life, a unique and very tough breed of people; we shall probably not meet their likes again.

Being tied up at the basin we decided to stay there for a couple of nights in order to explore the town. The narrow cobbled streets, and the very beautiful and original 17th century buildings intrigued us. When the Parliamentary Headquarters building was pointed out, we all pictured poor Steele and his Beeston Garrison, marching down the narrow street, being ridiculed as traitors and cowards. Our return journey was a much more relaxed affair, with a good horse there was no urgency and Joe was a good companion. He was a rough diamond and his language was coarse in the extreme. We wondered with his lack of education, whether he could read and write, we found out however that he was a worldly wise old man, who spoke a lot of common sense.

The trip was completed in easy stages and we stopped to explore the many villages, places of interest and generally enjoyed the pleasant Cheshire countryside. We were taken to climb the Hurleston Staircase in order to view the huge reservoir, which the council had insisted Telford provide with his Dee Water supply, for domestic use; this was insisted upon before they would give him permission to cut the canal over their land. This need he provided with a primitive but ingenious series of sluices, which allowed just the overflow to feed the reservoir, without jeopardizing his supply for the canal system. A study of that amazing man's achievement made us wonder how he managed to squeeze so much into his lifetime. As well as supervising the construction of a nationwide canal system, which included the Caledonian Canal, he was involved in canal building on the continent; he also built the awe inspiring Trevor Aqueduct. It was Telford who realised that an insufficient water supply could not maintain a broad gauge system, therefore he devised the narrow gauge lock, and so it is thanks to him that we have our narrow boat. He also turned his attention to our highway system, building the magnificent suspension bridges at Conway and Menai. He died aged just 77, practically having worked himself to death.

On the return journey we spent some time at Bunbury, renewing the friendship with the good blacksmith and Hardy took us to the ancient village church to view the amazing historic relics. Returning to Beeston the reunion between our old friend and the lock keeper was a pleasure to watch. Joe was full of praise for the way we looked after him, one comment being very significant, "Do you know" he said to his friend, "I think these lads have got a very good idea". I think that Ellis and Hardy were true pioneers of what has become today one of our major leisure industries enjoyed by a new breed of boat people, all be it much a more affluent breed.

From Beeston we were prepared for more bow hauling and so bade farewell to our old friend, but he would have none of it. "Not likely lads" he said, "I'm coming all the way back to Chester with you". We really had cultivated a firm friendship. With an early start the return trip to Chester was made by early afternoon, and I must admit that it was with heavy hearts that we descended the Northgate Staircase, to return to Tower Warf. As we moored Combermere for the final time, we noted that Joe had scurried off and quickly sought out the boatyard owner, they seemed to be well acquainted and were in deep conversation. Eventually the man came over and addressing Ellis he said, "Do you want her?" "What do you mean?" was the reply. "Combermere", said the man, "You can have her for a fiver; use her as your headquarters". "You can keep her here as long as you want,

I don't require any mooring fee". We were taken aback, but as the two worthies' plans were unfolded we suddenly realised why Joe had insisted on coming back to Chester with us. It appeared that the old man was living in dire poverty in Beeston and had looked upon our arrival as a ray of hope. He was prepared to move to Chester and if Ellis would permit, use our narrow boat as his living quarters. His friend would employ him breaking up the remaining barges, in the timber yard and in return for his accommodation Joe would keep the boat in good order acting as caretaker, there was also stabling available for his horse. To further persuade us the old couple emphasized that, as well as being our H.Q. the boat was always available with a horse at any time for canal trips.

We all got into a huddle on the towpath to discuss the proposal. The first objection to the idea came from Hardy who said that it was not feasible, because the canal was too far from Sandycroft for our weekly meetings. Opinions were expressed that the whole idea was more advantageous to the two old cronies than us. The fact was that a fiver probably represented the scrap timber value of our boat, without all the hard work. By employing Joe, the boat yard owner would escape that chore, plus, he would have a resident caretaker for his yard, but as far as Joe was concerned we were the answer to all his problems. On the other hand Ellis argued strongly in favour of the idea, he always had visions of a Sea Scout Troop, and saw this as the ideal opportunity. Finally, Hardy's viewpoint prevailed and so sadly, much to Joe's disappointment we had to turn down the offer. Subsequently, I have often questioned the wisdom of our decision:

What if: Ellis had purchased a Shropie Fly for a fiver?

What if: We had kept it in good order with attendant bargee and horse?

What if: Ellis had used it for visitor trips, would he have been a pioneer among the people who later re-developed the waterways?

What if: By waving a magic wand we could today have our Shropie Fly back at Tower Wharf, in pristine condition, what would be the return on that fiver investment?

Only dreams are made of ifs and buts, the reality was that we refused, and Combermere would end up on the canal side. Our dear old friend Joe would make his weary way back to Beeston to his Spartan existence but as a parting gift he was presented with the remains of our food stock. We knew he would make good use of it, as he was spending a night on board before his return. Farewells were said and as we made our long trek back to our homes and normality, I feel sure we were a better and wiser group of lads, thanks to our all too brief encounter with the Cut and its hardy and unique boat people.

Sandycroft Boyscouts Camping in 1932, with visiting sisters and friends

Scout troop with loaded trek cart in Broughton

High jinx at Broughton

Wash time at camp

Old Joe, Mitchy and Ron Westhead

The Reverend Hardcastle reading history

Negotiating the locks at Bunbury

Underway, towed by Dobbin the horse

Camping at Rhosesmor

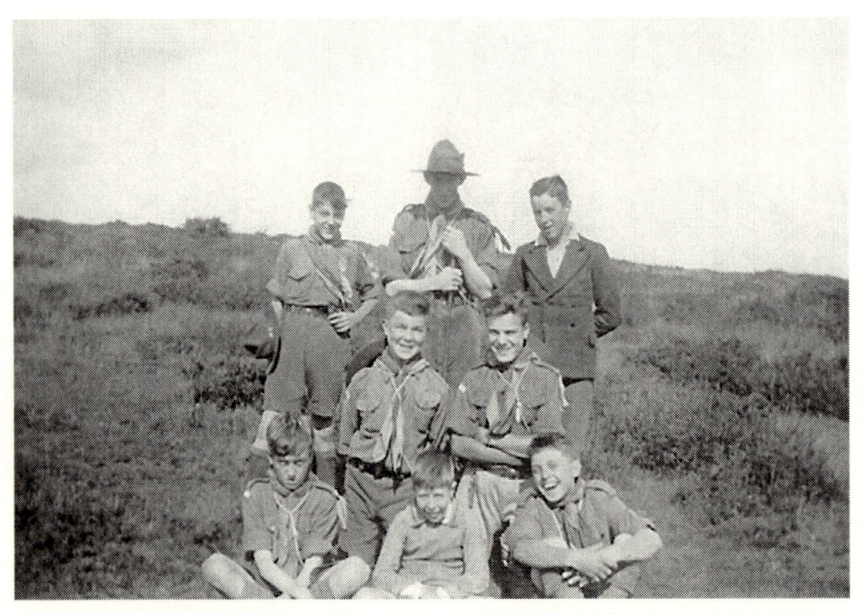

Exploring the hill fort on Moel y Gaer, Rhosesmor

On board Boswell's Rio speed wagon

Singing around the camp fire, me on the mouthorgan

Old Beeston Castle circa Prince Edward

Chapter 4

From Boy to Man

In 1932, at the age of 12 years, I had reached that great dividing point when back in our parents' school days the more academically minded moved on to grammar school while the remainder stayed on in "standard 6" until they found employment or reached the age of 14 years. How lucky we were that in 1930 a new educational concept had been introduced called Secondary Education and a new school had been built on Deeside to facilitate this, Deeside Central School. There were 20 places in the new school allotted to Cannon Drew School, 10 boys and 10 girls so Mr Davies our headmaster set a test (a simplified 11+) for the top class and as a result I became one of the fortunate few chosen.

What a wonderful occasion arriving at the brand new school where we found facilities only previously dreamed of. There were playing fields for football, cricket, hockey and netball and running tracks for athletics. The school was divided into three houses, Rowan, Beech and Cedar, I was in Rowan, each house had its own distinctive PT kit and the whole atmosphere was one of competitive pride. I was allocated to Standard 2C where our teacher was Mr Richard Morris, another Hawarden man like Maldwyn Davies. Mr Morris was a most wonderful person, a gifted and natural teacher who led by example. He had a marvellous way of dealing with children and could handle the most unruly. He was a good footballer and gave tuition to all us lads and he even formed a cycling club to take us all out exploring at the weekends. Dicky, as he was affectionately known, was my hero and throughout my life I have attempted to follow his example.

As I progressed through the school I enjoyed the facilities such as; music, where I joined the choir; art, taught by the renowned artist Mr Macalister Turner; woodwork, with Mr Lawson Gill. After three years I finally entered Standard 5 Commercial with teacher Miss Dilys Morris. Although I was making good progress my mind was constantly with my dad and the great struggle he had to raise the family. Eventually my mind was made up and I began the hunt for employment so that I could help out with the family budget.

With help from my elder sister Eileen I got a job in her place of work, Bees Nurseries, Sealand. I was to work in the shrub department for the weekly wage of 10 shillings, this was for a six day week and one penny was stopped for the Lloyd George[2] so take home pay was 9 shillings and eleven pence (9/11). That was a great help to the family, the rent was paid, I got 1 shilling and sixpence pocket money and mum had some left over towards the shopping bill.

At that time the owner of Bees Nursery was Mr Bully of Ness, a famous horticulturist, whose home is now Ness Gardens. The work was hard and we cycled there in all weathers, a good toughening up process, which did us no harm. After twelve months, at the age of 16 years, opportunity knocked and I was offered employment in Courtauld's Textile factory in Flint. This was via a contact in the Boy Scouts, Stan Cooper who worked in the office at Deeside Mill. The wage was a very handsome 18/6 but on shift work, so I made the move. I must admit that from the outset I absolutely hated every minute spent in the mill. The majority of the work force were male but there were a lot of girls

---

2   An early form of sickness benefit

of school leaving age who were exploited and bullied by the staff who were in the main Lancashire or Yorkshire folk.

Once again, in all weather, I cycled between Mancot and Flint; Crosville ran a bus service to the factory but that cost 2/6 per week so I cycled! My employment was in the Winding Department and the job was called "weighing in", this involved weighing the heavy trays of silk bobbins produced in the department and then transferring them on trucks to the Twisting Department for further process. This was a vital operation because it recorded mill production, but it was hard work. My colleague on that job was a happy-go-lucky young lady from Sandycroft, Betty Knight, a good friend who had a great sense of humour. We used to cycle to work together and I suppose it could be said that what made life bearable in that horrible mill was the wonderful camaraderie of all the young people working there.

From a very early age I had done what many youngsters did in the 1920's and 30's, created our own entertainment. By learning to play the harmonica, a group of us like-minded workmates used to meet after work in the canteen. We formed a band, purely for our own amusement, a girl named Doris (one of the girls "on the desk" with Betty) was a good pianist and joined us along with Eric Holloway, who had an accordion, we all used to thoroughly enjoy ourselves.

My Mum by this time had upgraded my pocket money to 2/6, so at the weekends I was able to go to Chester with my mates. Our favourite picture house was the Regal, it was brand new and they had a magnificent Compton organ, Horace Pilling played it and that was the main attraction, we loved listening to that. During these Saturday afternoons in Chester we used to love to go window-shopping, especially to Bowdlers in Boughton. Bowdlers were really pawnbrokers but always had a large display of harmonicas in the window. It was from Bowdlers that I purchased a Hohner cromatic for 7/6 and another lovely 3 octave instrument which allowed me to play bass in the band which cost me 4/6. As my weekly pocket money was only 2/6 it appears that I must have been a very thrifty lad.

During this time the war clouds were gathering over Europe as the Germans and Italians were threatening world stability. How well I recall that Saturday evening in September 1939; we were all sitting in a packed Regal and just as the show was about to start the manager came on stage to announce that the PM had declared war on Germany. The organ struck up and everybody stood up to sing "Land of Hope and Glory". That show of patriotism made me tingle from head to toe and such was the effect on me that on the following Monday I reported, along with several of my mates, to the recruiting centre in Chester. My preference was for the RAF and how delighted I was to be accepted there and then. I visualised being immediately called to fight for king and country but imagine my disappointment at being told to report back to work; they said that they would notify me when I was wanted! No escape from the mill then and of course in 1939 our country really was not prepared for war and quite a few months passed before I was finally called up.

On return to work we lads, who had volunteered, were formed into an air raid precaution group and we sandbagged vital areas of the factory and worked on the blackout so that we could operate at night. We also had to man the works tower as lookouts, to warn of air raids; this was a "voluntary" duty, which we did in rotation at night, unpaid. Eventually notification arrived for me to report to RAF Padgate for attestation. This was the ceremony of being "sworn in" and given your service number, it was also the selection board. It was here that I got my first taste of class distinction, which until that time I had no knowledge of, the first question was, "Which school did you go to?" My reply received a condescending look from the officer who probably thought that I would make an excellent wireless operator or rear gunner. I am sure that if I had said Kings School[3], I would have been recommended for higher things but as it was I was delighted with the outcome. I was going to have bird's eye view of the war; little did I know that as events unfolded I was still going to get my Worm's Eye View. Once again, imagine my frustration that, instead of being marched to the stores for kitting out and starting service life, I was given a small RAFVR[4] lapel

---

3   Then and now, a private school in Chester
4   Royal Air force Volunteer Reserve

badge and told, once again, to return to work and they would notify me when I was required; so it was back to the grind!

By this time the company had acquired an ancient fire engine and the works' fire brigade formed. I became part of the crew and spent a lot of time on that duty but eventually, after another couple of months dragged by; in August 1940 I finally got my calling papers. I was to report to the RAF recruiting centre in Blackpool, so having bid farewell to the Flint Mill and family and friends, I rolled into Blackpool Central Station on the troop train. We were quickly formed into squads of fifty and marched, in a fashion, into a large building near to Blackpool Tower where we were kitted out in uniform; now we had really joined up!

On leaving the station what an amazing sight greeted us, in every direction we saw nothing but Air Force blue, the whole town, from Squires Gate to Bisphan had been taken over by the RAF. It was one of the great secrets of the war; many thousands of men were trained there for the service. The billet I was allocated was no. 97 Palatine Road; there were a dozen young lads and a recruiting NCO in each billet, our officer proved to be a real fatherly figure. Sergeant "Taffy" Owen, an Anglesey man, was nicely settled in at the billet, having an arrangement with the landlady, Mrs Daly, a widow in her late 30's, the situation appeared to suit both parties very well!

At number 97, we lads had found a home from home, being well fed and cared for but from the Service point of view we were quickly thrown in at the deep end. Our squad was 2.A.14 (second wing, A squadron, 14 squad) and our drill sergeant was an ex Arsenal footballer, Sergeant Hockaday, and a cracker he was! The parade ground was the promenade from Squires Gate to Cocker Street and our spot was directly in front of the Metropole Hotel. Our spell of training there was a very short 12 weeks but in that time we probably gained a degree of efficiency which in peace time would have taken several years; it was that intensive. We were always on parade at first light where the order would be PT on the beach followed by an hours drill on the promenade, the rest of the day being taken up with our wireless operator training.

Morse training was carried out in the Winter Gardens, which had been completely equipped to handle several hundred at each sitting; we were blessed with an excellent tutor. All tutors were either ex GPO operators or retired merchant navy telegraphers our tutor Mr Zeal was the latter. He was a wonderfully patient man, thanks to him most of us made great progress. I always feel that I had a head start, having learned the rudiments of Morse code in the Boy Scouts. Our "tech" classes were held in a large room above Woolworths, the class involved the study of electricity and the fundamentals of radio reception and transmission as well as elementary insight into the use of signalling codes.

In training as a wireless operator there was no room whatsoever for failure; each week we had a Morse test in an exam room above Burton the Tailors on the sea front. We began at three words a minute and every week our test was one word faster, consequently anyone who failed the test was given a CT[5] slip and was immediately transferred to alternate training, only the successful survived.

As regards to our parade ground training, after a few short weeks Sgt Hockerday (known to us as Hockey) transferred us from being a civilian "rabble" into a smart efficient body of men who would have done credit to the Guards. Our drill was absolutely precise and he installed in us the belief that at the end of our twelve weeks at passing out parade we were going to get the award of "Smartest Squad". He assured us that if we achieved this goal he would see to it that we all got a weekend pass; what an incentive! So we all strove for perfection and in the Wireless Operator training I was determined to get through and not be CT'd like so many had. I loved every minute of that training and still have some of my old GEN books (containing information on anything to do with radio operating). The most rewarding thing of all though, was that I consistently achieved A1 passes.

Although these were seen as the "dark days" of the war, I can never recall any feeling of defeatism at Blackpool. Moral was sky high and a great sense of humour was always shining through, as when on parade one day Hockey said, "Are any of you lads interested in music? I want

---

5   Cease Training

half a dozen volunteers". Being a keen harmonica player I considered myself a musician and one of my billet mates, Eric Foster, was a good pianist so we put our hands up along with some others and the six of us were marched along to the squadron office in a hotel near to the tower. Imagine our consternation when we realised Hockey was bursting his sides laughing, as we were only required to move a piano from the hotel into a wagon to be taken for the use of a concert party!

However, all was not lost on the music front, as later on the Squadron Office notice board was an appeal by a Flight Sergeant Parsons. This was for any airmen interested in forming a Squadron Harmonica Band, the objective being to give charity concerts in church halls in the Blackpool area. Feeling sure that this was not just another way of taking the piss, I eagerly put my name forward and so opened a little chapter in my short Blackpool experience, which filled me with both happiness and pride. Within a few short days good old *Chief* Parsons had assembled about thirty keen lads and arranged for a room at HQ to be made available to us. We assembled each evening for practice and, hey presto, a band was formed. The repertoire he chose for us was mostly those lively *Savoy*[6] medleys, which were all the rage at that time and boy did we play those with some gusto!

In no time at all we had bookings all over the area and although we were a very unprofessional bunch our enthusiasm seemed to catch on and we had a good reception wherever we went. The good work we were doing soon got noted in high places and we were summoned to the Opera House for an audition to take part in the RAF show, Contact. This show was broadcast on the radio[7] each weekend but for security reasons it was always billed as "From Somewhere in England". Of course most of the people taking part were at that time training at Blackpool, the orchestra being conducted by Aircraftsman Sidney Torch and many others became household names[8]. For us the main thrill was sharing the stage with Aircraftsman George Formby who sang his whole range, including "Me Little Stick of Blackpool Rock",

---

6   Arranged by Carol Gibbons
7   From the Tower Ballroom
8   Charlie Chester, Max Miller

what a great privilege it was for us lads to tread the boards with such a celebrity.

In 1940 Walt Disney had produced his full-length cartoon films, Fantasia and Snow White and so during our morning parades, which were always long before daylight and during Black-out, we sang "Hi ho, hi ho, its off to Morse we go, we'll do our best to pass our test, hi ho, hi ho, hi ho", followed by a chorus of whistling. This was as we marched through the streets with the leading man in each squad carrying a white hurricane lamp and the man at the rear carrying a red one. What an hilarious carry-on, spirits were indeed very high. Another "little game" we used to play, with the co-operation of the service chiefs, was a ploy to fool the "fifth columnists" known to be active in the town. During the Passing Out Parades, watched by large crowds, as soon as we had passed the saluting base we all ran through the side streets to form up again at the rear of the parade to take a second salute. So if anybody was taking a count for transmission to the Reich, the figures would be very misleading!

As mentioned earlier, Hockey had been urging us on to become the Smartest Squad in A Squadron and after the big parade it was duly announced that we had achieved his objective. This of course caused great elation among the lads as we anticipated the promised reward. Imagine our feelings when on the next parade he told us that unfortunately the authorities had put a block on all leave and no one was allowed to leave Blackpool. What a bitter blow! Most of the lads who came from far afield reluctantly accepted the situation but as for myself, being a fairly local lad was furious. To think that I was so near home yet I could not nip to see the family; so I made my mind up, I was going to have a go! When I told Taff Owen this back in the billet he said, "Well good luck lad but remember, if you get caught, and there is every chance that you will, I will have to report you AWOL". We both shook hands on the deal.

With my haversack over my shoulder, I made my way to the main bus station where I had noticed buses leaving labelled Chester. I was soon in the correct queue, which was a long one, and got into conversation with a sergeant whom I discovered came from Frodsham. Suddenly, to my horror, I noticed that two SP's were checking everyone's passes and in panic I looked back but saw that they were also guarding the main doors, I was trapped! There was no way I could do a runner, Taff had been quite correct in his assessment of the situation, so I prepared to meet my punishment. I must have been shaking like a leaf because my new companion said, "What's the matter lad, haven't you got a pass?" I related my plight and the fact that I was determined to see my family and his response was to perform an act, which to my mind symbolised the comradeship, which existed in the forces in those trying times. He said, "Don't worry lad we will get you home, just put your right hand deep in my pocket (we both had greatcoats on) at this he put his left hand in. We got to the formidable figure of the sergeant SP and my companion whispered in his ear, immediately the SP asked us to follow him to the front of the queue where he then whispered into the bus conductor's ear, who then escorted us onto the bus and to the safety of a rear seat.

Once settled down on the bus I received a full explanation of what had just transpired. He had told the SP that I was a deserter from RAF Sealand and that he had been sent to arrest me, I was handcuffed and could they put us on the bus to save any embarrassment. As he left the bus at Frodsham my pal said, "Catch the 6pm bus from Queensferry tomorrow, I'll be waiting here and we will get back into Blackpool together. Because of that wonderful piece of quick thinking I was able to get a night at home in my very own bed and see my family, although I did not give them the details of how I managed to get there. The sergeant was as good as his word and we met as planned and got back into Blackpool with no problems.

All too soon our Blackpool days were over, but not before I had been befriended by a couple who had been at one of our concerts at their chapel. They made me welcome in their home and I kept in contact over the years and in fact in 1946 Mr & Mrs Garlick invited Dot and I to spend our honeymoon with them. So it was goodbye to Blackpool and on to my next posting in Yatesbury, Wiltshire to a wireless school for the training of aircrew. It was there that we advanced from 12 words per minute to 18 WPM and a lot of the training was in D H Rapides (flying classrooms). We now all wore a white flash on our caps, which indicated that we were aircrew undertaking training and were promoted to the rank of LAC. The one thing that stays in my mind though, is that in nearby Calne was the Harris bacon factory and I think we must have had the bulk of their production because the bacon and egg breakfasts at the camp were out of this world.

With the completion of my basic training the next posting was to No. 15 Service Flying Training School at Kiddlington, Oxfordshire. This station operated Airspeed Oxfords in which, pilots, navigators, engineers, W/Ops and air gunners were trained to meet operational standards. From the outset things did not go well as on the night of our arrival the aerodrome suffered a devastating air raid; this was at the tail end of the Battle of Britain when the Germans had resorted to night raids only. The station did round the clock training and at night the pilots used to practice circuit and bumps. Flare paths in those days were primitive Duck lamps that were lit and extinguished by flare path parties but on this particular night something had gone wrong with the air raid warning system. The station was "pounced on" by a flight of ME 110's, probably the best machines in service at the time. Two hangars and all aircraft in them were destroyed; the runway was pitted with bomb craters and three mobile aircraft were shot down, all crew lost. As a result, all trainees were given a fortnight leave while the station was put back in order.

It was while on that leave that Dot and I met in a friend's house in Hawarden. Dot was living and working in Liverpool with her grandmother at the time and was visiting her mum, dad and sister Ivy (now known as Babs) who had been evacuated to Mancot and then moved to Sandycroft. On the night we met Dot had been detained in Mancot on account of an air raid over Shotwick that had resulted in road closures. Had she left for home as usual we would not have met, so we had the Germans to thank for our chance meeting. A few days later Dot and I arranged to go for a walk in the Hawarden area and as night fell there was an air raid on Deeside (it was probable that they had been looking for our local airfield), Queensferry was hit with fatalities in Dundas Street and the Co-op store in Pentre was also hit. We panicked as our mothers were together in nearby Sandycroft; we ran all the way there to check that they were safe. As we dashed in to the house, under the kitchen table we could see the two unconcerned ladies were sitting knitting with cushions on their heads. It took more than an air raid to upset our mums!

Suddenly things took a drastic turn in my service life because upon my return to Kiddlington I discovered that my name was up on DRO's[9] for an overseas posting, I was to report to RAF Padgate! Why my wartime service took this sudden turn was a complete mystery at the time and only became apparent a couple of months later on my arrival in the Middle East. The intervening period however, was one of great importance and had a great impact on my life, I learned so many lessons about human nature and got involved in mutinous and high spirited adventure on the high seas.

---

9   Daily Routine Orders

The Late Mr Stephen Morris

Deeside School Gardeners 1930 Mr Morris on far right

Deeside Central School, class of 1932

Clocking on machine at Cortauld's Textile Factory

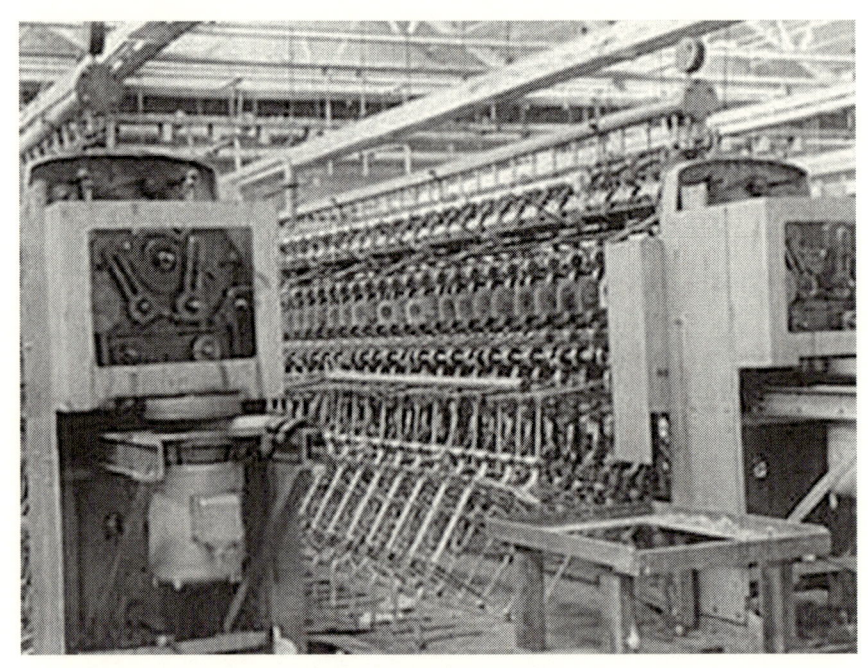

The winding machine

Silk bobbins on the coning machine

Deeside Mill fire station

Demolition showing the pillbox lookout tower

RAF Training Payslip

RAF Training Squad September 1940

RAF Padgate awaiting posting to the Middle East

Cover of the Contact Concert Party Programme featuring our Harmonica Band

CAFE IMPERIAL
69 71, TALBOT ROAD, BLACKPOOL
Parties Catered for.   Board and Accommodation.
Licensed.
SQUAD PARTIES SPECIALLY CATERED FOR.
Rooms for parents visiting at week-ends.
Terms : 7/6 Bed and Breakfast, 12/6 Full Board.

OFFICERS OF HIS MAJESTY'S F
become ME
THE
BLACKPOOL
76, TOPPING STREET.
Open - - - 12-0 noo
Sundays - - - 12-0

By Appointment

GIEVES Ltd.

80, PICCADILLY,

Royal Air Forc
Outfitters.

Temporary Address :

15a, CHURCH STREET,
BLACKPOOL.

"CON

Produced by F/LT. BRUCE SIEVIER, M.C.

1. A/C MILLER and Company ... "Out of the Blue"
   Compere—S/Ldr. K. L. WARRINGTON

2. THE RAFTAPPERS .... " Toy Trumpet "

3. Sergt. HILES and Corpl. McINDOE Comedy Acrobats

4. Flt./Sergt. PARSONS and his Harmonica Band
   Pianoforte A/C TRAILL

5. A/C AUSTIN .... "The Spider"

6. HELEN BREEN—Guest Artist

7. ALEC MUNRO .... Scottish Comedian

INTERVAL
SIDNEY TORCH and Orchestra

Devised and C
S/LDR. K. L. W
Orchestra under the directi
Orchestrations by
Stage Manager ....
Assist. Stage Manager ....
Stage Accompanist ....
Press Representative ....
Box Office Manager............

The Entertainment Committee th
Butson and the Tower Company, f

BRITANNIA VALET SERVICE
33, BOLTON STREET (corner shop).

ALL FORCES AND CIVIC ALTERATIONS
WHILE - U - WAIT.

Contact Page 1

ORCES are cordially invited to MBERS of **AERO CLUB** Tel. 4079. —1-0 p.m., 3-0—10-0 p.m. —2-0 p.m., 7-0—10-0 p.m.	FOR ALL YOUR **SPORTS REQUISITES** especially FOOTBALLS YOU OUGHT TO VISIT **R H. O. HILL'S** " Blackpool's Busiest Store "

"TACT"

● Business Manager - F/LT. D. H. SIMMONS.

8. ANITA .... Irish Songs

9. A.C BROWELL .... Conjuror and Ventriloquist

10. A.C TRACHY .... Female Impersonator

11. LUCILLE and MARIE ...... The sweet sophisticates

12. GEORGE FORMBY—as himself

FINALE .... " Out of the Blue "

Compered by
ARRINGTON
t of A/C SIDNEY TORCH.
EORGE RECORD.
.... Flt. Sgt. TURNBULL
.... A/C MONTY BERMAN
.... A/C LEN STEVENS
.... A/C COLIN NEIL MACKAY
.... A/C ANSELL
think Mr. J. H. Clegg, Mr. Clem
fo their kindness and co-operation.

JACK HEYWORTH Ltd.

CHURCH STREET,
BLACKPOOL.

The Musical Instrument Dealers.

We supply and service the R.A.F. Station Dance Band. Large stocks of musical instruments on sale free of purchase tax.

We also buy Pianos, Clarinets, Saxes, Trumpets, Drums, String Basses, Accordions, etc.

CASH WAITING.

Your instruments will be valued free of charge by Jack Heyworth, Britain's acknowledged valuer of musical instruments.

OFFICERS' KIT MADE TO ORDER. All Accessories in Stock

Military Tailor — *George Ash* LIMITED — Army R.A.F.

64-66, CHURCH STREET, BLACKPOOL. (Tel. 595.)

Contact Page 2

Contact Back Cover

Chapter 5

The Jock Experience

I suddenly found myself back at Padgate with a large overseas draft and what a rabble we proved to be. Some 2000 strong, we were split into squads of 50; try to picture the scene, so many reluctant bodies assembled on the parade ground twice a day supposedly under the control of a group of desperate NCO's. The problems of the NCO's were further confounded by the actions of a character, which later became known as "The Phantom", how he actually performed we were never really able to grasp. He would float around the squads and just when the NCO had established some kind of order, a high-pitched voice would echo across the parade, "Order", he would shout. Each time this resulted in complete chaos as 2000 men burst with laughter and broke ranks. I can still picture warrant officer in charge, his face blue with rage, shouting, "Catch that F****** man, I'll have his guts for garters". That man, Jock Handley, was never caught; he endeared himself to all of us and was the type of character who made wartime service life bearable, nobody would have ever dreamed of shopping Jock. He was a man with a most wonderful sense of humour, he insisted on the use of his nickname of Jock, although he was not a Scot but in fact a Brummy from Stoke on Trent. He was much older than the rest of us, probably in his late thirties at the time, and he held the lowest possible rank in the RAF, AC2 GD. He had no ambition for promotion but we were to find out that he was a great example to us all and a natural leader.

My first personal encounter with Jock was when he formed an Escape Committee! Padgate at that time was a high security camp, surrounded by a ten-foot perimeter fence and anyone on overseas draft was strictly confined, no leave whatsoever! Jock did not agree with this arrangement! How, in such a short time, he organised this we never knew but he let it be known that any lads who lived locally and would like a spot of leave were to report to his hut; I duly reported. The organisation inside that hut was a measure of the man; he sat at a table, a ledger in front of him, surrounded by the other members of his "committee" who were also AC2's. All details of each "escapee" were recorded, service number, squad number, nickname, home address etc. When I told him that I did not have a nickname but that my surname was Donnell and my first name was Harold, he retorted, "Good God, sounds like the Battle of Hastings", and he entered as my nickname, Don. That is how my nickname came about and is still used today 66 years later and all thanks to Jock.

I was reassured not to worry about parades as he had my squad number and the last three of my service number. That was all we had to listen out for when the corporal was taking roll and upon hearing it you just replied, "Corporal". So Jock and his group would float around and at the appropriate moment would do the honours, so I would not be missed. The next detail was regarding the escape; Jock's hut was in a corner of the camp, quite close to a housing estate and in that corner were some dense bushes extending to the perimeter fence. In that thicket a portion of the wire fence had been carefully cut with wire cutters and then secured with hooks, this meant that they could be folded back for an easy exit and then the hooks re-fastened before your hasty getaway. He also furnished me with details of the nearest bus stop for a Chester bound service. I was to report for escape duty at fifteen hundred hours as the Chester bus was due at fifteen thirty. The following day I was to be back before 23.59 where I would return to camp via the main gates, as bold as brass! The escape route was to be used for exit only as there was no check by the guardroom on the main gate as anybody entering the camp was assumed to be permanent staff.

With all of this information noted, I returned to Jock's hut at the appropriate time to find him earnestly looking out of the window. He explained that the perimeter guards, who patrolled the camp, passed by every five minutes rounding the corner just after the bushes and so would be out of sight at the precise moment that he whispered, "Off you go, remember to re-fasten the wire fence". By now I was feeling quite the expert at this kind of leave-taking and within a couple of hours I was home with the family. I took Dot into Chester where we duly became engaged, without a lot of ceremony and following that brief encounter we were not to see each other again for four long years. So once again, "Thank you Jock".

Within a few days we were all packed and ready for embarkation, now with the addition of Tropical Kit we had a full and heavy kit bag to carry on the march, we all felt like pack mules! Under strict orders we silently left the camp in the early hours and were marched to the railway station to entrain for our trip to Gourock, port of Glasgow where part of the convoy was assembling. The next day we drew up alongside our troopship, SS Almanzora, she had been a merchant cruiser in the battle of Jutland and was to be our home for the next month. We were first relieved of our kit, which was stored in the hold as "not wanted on voyage" and so, armed with just our side kit we boarded the vessel looking for C deck, to which we had been allocated. Imagine our consternation as we went down one companionway after another to arrive, finally, at C deck deep in the bowels of the ship! It was pretty near the water line and what a hell hole, there was very little light as the portholes were blacked out and there was no ventilation system. In peacetime this had been the third class dining room and now some 500 of us were squeezed in, the whole deck area had been cleared and 20, long wooden tables and benches had been screwed down on the deck and hooks had been fitted to the deck head on which to sling 10 hammocks. This was to be home to us, we ate and slept right there, 25 men to each table for eating and as for sleeping, ten used the hammocks the rest either slept on the tables or the deck itself.

Such conditions could have been demoralising but not a bit of it! We were of course destined to have a worm's eye view as the hierarchy had cabins on "A" deck but we had the trump card in the form of Jock. Throughout the entire voyage he had us all in stitches and in his own inimitable style, created havoc for any form of authority. However, to add insult to injury, if our living quarters were appalling then the food served up was disgusting. The party working in our galley were a gang of stevedores from Liverpool who, by their own admission, had volunteered because they thought it was going to be a cushy number. One thing for sure, cooks they were not, from the outset I had offered to be a mess orderly which entailed going into the galley with a dixie to collect the rations and then dish them out. A typical main meal would be pieces of meat of doubtful origin which were as tough as old boots accompanied by potatoes boiled in their jackets but the navvies could not even be bothered to wash them before hand and they would be served up with mud and all. Having had enough of this, Jock decided to take action and said, "Lads, take that rubbish back to the galley and tell them that we refuse to eat it". The reaction was immediate! It must have been reported to the upper decks as suddenly a figure appeared at the top of the companionway; it was the RAF orderly officer who was unbelievably attired in Safari gear and sporting golfing socks and a monocle. At the sight of him Jock suddenly let out, "Bloody Hell, Claude Hulbert"! Ignoring the remark the officer said, "I say RAF, this is not good enough you know". The response was immediate; some of the lads grabbed the rotten potatoes left on the table and pelted him with them. He beat a very hasty retreat and must have reported to the officer in command that we had trouble down below.

Following all this Jock said, "Stick to your guns lads, and not a word". We had obviously caused a stir among the powers that be and we did not have to wait long for the next development. First, we heard a distant bugle call followed by the clatter of marching feet down the metal companionway. Suddenly, on the spot previously occupied by the RAF orderly officer there stood the magnificent figure of non other than the Ship's Master at Arms, the man responsible for discipline on the troopship. He was a Regimental Sergeant Major and was accompanied by two Military Policemen; they were the epitome of "spit and polish", all highly polished brass, white Blanco and red sashes and one of them held the bugle. Now, I do not know whether Windsor Davies was one of our members but I feel sure that the character he portrayed after the war in "It Ain't Half Hot Mum" must have been based on this particular Sergeant Major. His first bellowed outbreak was, "Right, you 'orrible little men, 'shun'!" As we got to our feet he then shouted, "What do you think you're doing? Orderlies, report to the galley to collect your food." Not a man moved. Now, his face distorted with rage, he produced a copy of the King's Regulations from under his arm. From this, he loudly read the section that related to 'Mutiny on the High Seas'. This detailed the terrible punishment that could be inflicted on mutineers, including being clapped in irons, flogged or even keel hauled. Closing the book he then asked, "Have you got a spokesman?" We knew that if anyone had stepped forward he would have been clapped in irons. Not a man moved but I heard Jock remark under his breath, "He will have to go!" The sergeant major, his face now blue with rage, let go with a torrent of abusive and foul language in regard to what he thought of us all, his final remark being, "God help Blighty if we depend on you lot!" When the fearsome figure had departed, Jock addressed us all saying, "Good work lads, we've got 'em, let's see what happens next, they can't clap us all in irons."

By now our action must have had the officer class in utter confusion, they did not know how to handle it. Their next move however, turned out to be a 'God Send', literally because in their desperation they sent down the Padre! When this good man arrived and asked what was our problem, we all breathed a sigh of relief, as we knew we could trust a man of the cloth. Immediately Jock went forward and explained to him the root cause of our action and upon hearing the full story the padre said, "OK, boys, what do you suggest?" This was just up Jock's street and he replied, "We should kick all those scallywags out of the galley, get them to scrub the decks or something and we will do our own cooking." "What an excellent idea" said the padre, "I'll suggest that it is my solution to punish you all." Immediately orders came from above to this effect and as we had several 'cooks' amongst us, we all took it in turn to do our cookhouse chores. From that moment on the food was great but Jock's remark of 'He will have to go' had a far-reaching effect for that unfortunate sergeant major!

During all this time we had been confined below decks as the convoy was passing through 'U-boat Alley' but once clear and in the mid-Atlantic, we were at least allowed up on deck. At last we could see the huge convoy of which we were a part, it was a massive collection of eighty troop and supply ships escorted by 120 warships. We were able to study and marvel at the efficiency of our convoy system as this large fleet was manoeuvred with clockwork precision, radio silence was observed and all communication was via signalling lamp and as we were wireless operators we could read all the messages. Our admiration for the Royal Navy knew no bounds; our convoy got through on account of its sheer strength and we constantly heard the rumble of depth charges from our escorting destroyers. The U-boats never got amongst us and any reconnaissance aircraft that ventured near beat a hasty retreat, as the sky was black with anti-aircraft fire. After about ten days the convoy put into Freetown for refuelling and while we were anchored there in the huge bay we saw an American ship come in. It was in the evening and it was all lit up and had the 'stars and stripes' and the words AMERICA painted in bold letters on her side. America was still neutral at that time but clearly visible on deck was a crated cargo of aircraft and she had sailed across the Atlantic like that! One of our lads remarked, "The Yanks want the best of both worlds."

While in Freetown the usual 'bum boats' came along side, passing fruit and souvenirs up via their baskets on a rope while the young lads dived in the crystal clear waters to retrieve the money thrown in as payment. However one of our 'wigs' cruelly threw in a penny wrapped in silver paper and we soon learned that the youngsters had a good command of English swearwords! Soon our convoy was underway again and heading for South Africa and despite our cramped and confined quarters we had great fun in the evenings. After 'turning in' Jock would always give his rendition of Stanley Holloway monologues (he knew them all) and 'Little Nell' poems, made famous by Billy Cotton. He would have us all 'bursting our sides' and there is no doubt, had we been torpedoed at that time we would have all gone down laughing.

As we got into the South Atlantic life below became unbearable, so in the evenings we were allowed to bring our hammocks up on deck where there were facilities for hanging them; that was wonderful. Through the grapevine we discovered that our main escorts were the brand new battleship, "Prince of Wales" and the old battle cruiser, "Repulse"; it is well-recorded history of course, regarding the fate of those two magnificent ships. It was during this period of our voyage that one of the cruisers, HMS Devonshire, was detached from the convoy to go in search of the German armed cruiser, SS Atlantis which was wreaking havoc with our shipping, carrying out hit-and-run raids. However, we soon had the news that Devonshire had caught and sank the raider.

We were now destined for Cape Town and Durban where the convoy was to split up, one half going to India and Singapore and our half going to Egypt. It was during this part of the voyage that Jock was hatching his next episode, to disrupt life for the authorities! Things went quietly until we docked and were on our way to Durban when all the time I was thinking, "What is a trainee Air-gunner doing on this overseas draft?" Our arrival at Durban was a memorable one, as our ship tied up; we were all entertained on the dockside by the "Lady in White". She was a famous opera singer who used to perform over a microphone for each ship, what a wonderful voice she had! I cannot recall her name but it was a real experience to listen to her.

We had a few days shore leave in South Africa to do some exploring but all too soon we were underway again with our half of the convoy proceeding up the East African coast. My most vivid memory is of our two main escorts, Prince of Wales and Repulse, sailing between our lines of ships with the marine bands playing in a final, fateful farewell; they then continued to escort the Far Eastern section of the convoy. It was at that time that Jock put his final plan into action, the one he promised when he said that the Master at Arms had to go. We had no idea how he was going to achieve the downfall of such a formidable opponent. By this time some kind of democratic order had been established because once a week, we ordinary troops were allowed into the first class lounge to play Crown and Anchor, the for-runner of Bingo. Needless to say, Jock was very scornful of this concession and duly, a note was pinned to the ship's notice board in the lounge announcing that THE SHITTER WILL STRIKE TONIGHT IN THE CROWN AND ANCHOR BOWL. Everyone, from the Ships Officers to the rabble on C deck was completely baffled by what this meant. The answer soon came to light, when next morning a large sample of human excrement was found in the said bowl. How had he done it? Nobody ever found out but the result was very amusing and all of the men on board the ship were roaring with laughter, except that is, the Master at Arms! He had an idea that the trouble had originated on C deck so he ordered all of us to parade in the first class lounge. There he resorted, in his usual furious way, to lay into the lot of us using unrepeatable language and ending with the threat that if he caught the "Shitter" he would have his guts for garters.

Having accomplished the first part of his plan Jock set about the final humiliation and on the notice board appeared THE SHITTER WILL STRIKE TONIGHT ON THE MASTER AT ARMS CABIN DOORSTEP. Can you imagine the reaction? The whole ship was shaking with laughter. Half of the troops on board were a Royal Artillery regiment and these lads were used for guard duties, mostly guarding the corridors of the officers' cabins. As a result of the threat, the sergeant major doubled the guard but Jock had them all eating out of his hand because the next morning his mission had been completed. The response was hilarious, nobody, except us lads, knew the identity of the "Shitter" but everywhere we went on board everyone was laughing about the episode. The sergeant major was reduced to a foul-mouthed, gibbering imbecile and for the rest of the voyage he confined himself to his cabin, whether he ever recovered we don't know.

Our next port of call was Aden, for refuelling and once again a few hours of shore leave but the immediate area was a dump that we were glad to get away from. Here our convoy broke up and each ship made an individual dash up the Red Sea for Port Tewfic. It had to be dash at that time as the Germans had a fair amount of air supremacy and were carrying out shipping raids from their bases in Tripolitania. We made a brief stop in Port Sudan to drop off troops but on leaving we had a mighty scare. We were underway when a mighty explosion shook the whole ship. We all prepared to make a dash for it thinking that we had been torpedoed but to our relief found that the artillery boys had just fired a practice round! From our main 4 inch gun on the stern we all saw plumes of water some half a mile away. Thankfully that was the only time that they carried out a practice, as I don't think the old girl could have stood up to any more! Very soon we were all disembarking at Tewfic, and non-too soon from what we were to learn later. Almanzora was hit during an air raid the following evening, although she did survive to see the war out.

All too soon we all found ourselves incarcerated in another transit camp, a la Padgate, this time Kasfarit in the Canal Zone. Now attired in tropical kit but still shuffling around in squads of 50 in the midst of the usual RAF disorganisation, the entire camp was under canvas and through here passed all troops who were arriving in Egypt to be moved to their designated units. Of course, the unit had not experienced an intake like ours before and with some difficulty we were herded into a kind of orderly parade to be addressed by a very bronzed Warrant Officer (I/C Parade). This very confident disciplinarian firstly informed us that we were 'orrible little men, who needed to get their knees brown and then proceeded to tell us of all the horrors that lay ahead of us in this foreign country. Suddenly, across the parade ground echoed the high-pitched cry of ORDER!! He was at it again, drifting from one squad to another. The very lordly warrant officer bellowed to his NCO's, "Catch that bloody man, I'll have his guts for garters". Where had we heard that expletive before?

That ghostly cry echoing across the desert sands was the last I ever heard of Jock and I often wonder what became of him. Of one thing we can be certain, wherever he went he would create havoc! Most of us often wondered, with him coming from Stoke on Trent, was his name really Handley? Maybe it was just another twist of his sense of humour but one thing we were certain of was that he was a very courageous and unselfish man who would do anything to help his comrades. He was also a great moral booster; there was only one true Jock Handley. That unique individual with a delightful sense of humour was a constant thorn in the side of authority. His main dislike was military discipline, which he always referred to as bullshit. I don't know whether the powers that be, in desperation, offered him to Rommel by posting him up The Blue but I am certain that if he ever became a prisoner he would have driven them up the wall and probably have shortened the war by twelve months!

Almanzora in Peacetime colours

Empress of Russia in Convoy (taken from a porthole of Almanzora!)

Chapter 6

Up "The Blue"

Our time at Kasfarit was short indeed and our draft was quickly split up and dispatched to various units throughout the Middle East. It now became apparent why we had been sent to this particular theatre of war as twenty of us wireless operators found ourselves at Helwan, some twenty miles south of Cairo. We were to be part of a special service unit and when comparing notes we discovered that we were all in the same boat, having all trained at Blackpool for aircrew and all having gained good passes and came to the conclusion that this was why we were selected for this particular mission.

At this stage of the war the Germans were creating havoc with our communications systems with the introduction of the ENIGMA machine. Their signalling system and coding system was far in advance of ours and was threatening to be a deciding factor in the outcome of the war. Under the leadership of General Auchinlech, the re-organised 8th army had just launched a brilliant counter attack against Rommel's Africa Corp Panzer divisions[10] and inflicted the first defeat of the German Army. The Libyan battlefield was littered with abandoned

---

10   This was code named Operation Crusader

enemy equipment and we were on hand at just the right moment; who said that the British always do too little too late?

FLT/LT Maskell, who we soon nicknamed "Dan" as Dan Maskell had been a Wimbledon Champion, commanded the SSU that was being hurriedly assembled at Helwan. Our senior NCO's were Warrant Officer Dole, known to one and all as "Shag" as this was the name he addressed everyone, what a wonderful character he was; the other NCO was Sgt (Chalky) White. These two were *time expired* men who had volunteered for the unit in preference to going home to Blighty and how invaluable their contribution was to be. The unit was approximately 50 strong with a good selection of skills, many were wireless mechanics with a wide knowledge of engineering but about a dozen were rather well heeled, mystery men. These dozen were LAC's like us but who spoke rather *far back*; we subsequently gathered that they had been sent out with Dan (from Bletchley Park) to lead the unit in the search for ENIGMA equipment.

We took delivery of 20 US Army GMC, six-wheel-drive wagons, the very best there was and far superior to anything we possessed at that time. Our first duty was to drive a wagon around a circuit of petrol drums to entitle us to be issued with a driver's licence. W/O Dole exploded when I told him that I could not drive. "Get in the driving seat, Shag" he said, "Every man in this unit drives". The good old lad got in the cab with me, explained the rudiments and as I made the circuit without too much grinding of gears, issued me with my first driving licence!! Our next move was to the clothing stores where we were all issued with Army Khaki Battle Dress and equipment; gone the RAF blue. Our officers were liaising with the unit of the Long Range Desert Group (LRDG) who were going to help co-ordinate our operation. We now had to load large quantities of petrol onto the wagons; each was half loaded with 10-gallon tins. These tins were made of paper-thin metal, many of which leaked, anyone who served in the ME would know of these, they were nothing like Gerry cans! We also had to take sufficient rations with us including large quantities of water for a long operation. How lucky I was that once again I was part of a small unit, in the Jack Hanley style, where comradeship was paramount and in which self-discipline of the highest order prevailed.

And so we set off into action, leaving Cairo behind we headed west through the Egyptian Western desert, heading for Libya. At night we were glad to sleep in the back of our wagons, despite the strong smell of petrol, to cook and brew up we had to keep well clear of the cans! After a couple of days we arrived at Buq Buq, the point from which the army had launched its offensive and from there we had to follow the Diamond Track. This was the route the army sappers had cleared through the minefield and was marked about every mile by a post, which had a tin diamond, nailed to the top; these diamonds were made from empty petrol tins. We had two despatch riders with the unit whose job it was to scout ahead finding each diamond pole to guide the convoy through. However, the best-laid plans can go wrong, as soon after setting out we ran into the most appalling weather. It was later stated to have been the worst weather ever recorded in the region. It was the Khamseen season but in addition to violent sand storms we encountered torrential rain and vast areas of the desert were turned into a morass. Khamseen is Arabic for 50 and it was said that these winds could last for that number of days, trust us to be in the Western Desert just then!

During this storm our wagons, equipment and us were plastered in mud and this of course put our diamond routers out of action, as they had to travel in the back of the wagons. Having great difficulty in finding the route the convoy was lost for a while but that was where Shag and Chalky proved their worth. They were experienced in navigating by compass and thanks to their help we were able to pass through the minefields safely. After many gruelling miles we eventually came to *Musso Wire*, an elaborate barricade of barbed wire, which the Italians had erected along the entire Libyan frontier from Halfaya deep into the Sahara; we passed through a section cleared for tanks. Although we got the convoy safely through the wire, the weather conditions were still atrocious with the abnormal mixture of sand and rainstorms. We were virtually travelling blind. So just a few miles inside the frontier Dan decided to call a halt and camp down for the night.

We had formed our wagons into a defensive circle and sat tight, waiting for the storm to abate. It was a regular feature of these Khamseen gales that as night approached the dust-laden wind would die down, leaving a perfectly clear night sky. So it was and on our first night in Libya the air was crystal clear and the heavens ablaze with stars. It was Christmas Eve and Dan had issued us all with a bottle of beer and so we all gathered around to sing a few carols accompanied by myself on the mouthorgan. Later we had our first desert survival lesson from the Old Sweats[11], how to make a portable cooking stove. This device was used by all troops in the Western desert; you simply took an empty petrol tin and filled it with petrol soaked sand, this was then lit to give a nice steady heat, sufficient to make a brew and cook a makeshift meal.

Our meal that Christmas eve was corned beef hash, a mixture of corned beef and hard tack biscuits, mashed and boiled together and washed down with a bottle of Stella beer. To round off our celebration, as we looked north, we were treated to a wonderful firework display. The sky was full of what appeared to be skyrockets and lots of *bangers* were lighting up the desert. As we learned later though, this was not someone celebrating; a section of the German Afrika Corp had been surrounded and cut off near Fort Capuzzo and at that moment were being paid a nightly visit by Wellingtons from the Canal Zone. Obviously, those poor blighters were not enjoying a peaceful Christmas Eve as we were.

For the next couple of days, although we had occasional sandstorms, the elements seemed to have pity on us and we were able to pick our way from diamond to diamond again, eventually to arrive at El Adem. This was a very important landing ground and a key point in the Libyan Campaign. It was a very flat area on a high escarpment, some 20 miles inland from Tobruk. It commanded a tremendous view and the Italians had put in a lot of work here in constructing excellent runways. There were lots of wrecked and abandoned German and Italian aircraft everywhere; many had been used as anchorage for tents, a safeguard against destruction by sandstorm. El Adem was now established as Advanced Headquarters, Western Desert (AAHQ W/D) and this was where Dan was to set up his HQ for our operation.

---

11   Experienced desert soldiers

As ours was of course, a rather secret mission, all movement was carried out in complete radio silence and to achieve this Dan's first acquisition was a German BMW motorbike, from which he had removed the sidecar and machine gun. Using this vehicle he was able to co-ordinate our search for enemy radio equipment; Dan was certainly a C/O who led from the front! From these headquarters Dan was to liaise with the LRDG[12] regarding all possible search sights and just a word here about that elite unit is appropriate: In my opinion, they were the bravest and most fearless desert troops, most had been recruited from the Brigade of Guards and were the eyes and ears of the Eighth Army. Their origin dated back to T E Lawrence in World War 1 but in the 1920's our army had developed the use of motor vehicles in place of camels and had fully explored Egypt's Western Desert and Northern Sahara, becoming familiar with all tracks connecting oasis. With all this invaluable information they were able to operate behind enemy lines during Rommel's occupation of Libya and also set up viewing posts from which to observe all activity. It was this knowledge that they were going to pass on to Dan and I feel greatly honoured that for just a short while, we were associated with this gallant band of men.

An amusing incident, which occurred at AAHQ, is I think worth mentioning. A supply ship had arrived at Tobruk and amongst its cargo was an invaluable NAAFI wagon, these used to travel between units in the War Zone and when it arrived it was always a case of first come, first served. El Adem had this commanding view of the Tobruk track of course and so when a vehicle was spotted in a cloud of dust, the cry went up, "NAFFI wagon ho!" and everyone tore down the escarpment to meet it, all hoping to be first in the queue because in no time it would be sold out. Now, I think that the biggest and strongest member of the HQ was the C/O, Air Commodore Beemish, a great bull of a man, sporting a flaming red beard. No one could outpace Beemish, he arrived at the wagon when it was about half a mile away from the unit and it continued to roll slowly on as the men arrived forming a running queue with a smiling Beemish in front. This procession continued until reaching the landing ground and once again we had a prime example of an officer leading from the front!

---

12   Long Range Desert Group

Very soon Dan began to sort us out and designate our potential targets. The first group that I was joined had two wagons and we were to report to the 2nd South African Division, responsible for the *fireworks* and surrounding the Germans at Fort Capuzzo! They had a couple of likely sites for us to explore where some German radioactivity had been observed and also where an Italian plane had recently been forced to land quite near to the German perimeter. At the time, we were still getting our fair share of daily sandstorms, which kept everyone's heads down and so during these periods we were able to roam freely in our search. However we were in an area of uncharted minefields and encountered our first mishap. The accompanying wagon, driven by Cpl Basham and LAC Bob Chisholm, struck a mine and was a complete loss. Fortunately, apart from Bob having a slight head wound nobody else was injured.

This first venture of ours, at Fort Capuzzo, was to prove fruitless and a complete failure. The following day, under the cover of a sandstorm and while the other lads were in the South African Lines, Stan Wainwright (from Shrewsbury) and I decided to go out into No Mans Land and investigate the Italian Fighter. When we found it can you imagine our frustration on discovering that, apart from not having any high tech equipment in the cockpit to give us any coding clues, it did not even have a radio! It was like a World War 1 plane, such was Mussolini's preparedness for war! At that precise moment, with us in a very vulnerable position, the sandstorm decided to abate! As Stan and I went to ground beneath the aircraft, there was a sudden burst of tracer fire from the enemy lines, which struck our wagon carrying its valuable but dangerous load of petrol! Within seconds it was a blazing wreck as we kept our heads down under the aircraft. Fortunately there was no further fire from the enemy, the Germans must have been satisfied with their achievement and did not want to waste valuable ammunition on two stupid lads looking at this useless Italian aircraft!

To me, the most upsetting thing about the loss of our wagon was the fact that on board, in my kit bag were my very precious mouth organs, which I had purchased as a youngster and had enjoyed playing for a sing-along. Strangely enough, they were Hohner instruments, made in Germany and I have never forgiven the Germans for depriving me of the enjoyment they brought! However, I cannot speak too highly of the South Africans, they were quick to get us back to their lines and for a couple of days we were all treated to some excellent hospitality. They kept us well fed and supplied us with a tent and lots of blankets for comfort. Despite this, we were all really quite worried, having drawn an absolute blank and we had lost two very valuable wagons and cargo, what was Dan going to say?

A few days later Dan had got wind of our plight and sent out a recovery party to take us back to El Adem. On confronting our C/O all fears were allayed, as we rediscovered his qualities as an excellent leader. Having listened patiently to our explanations of exactly what had happened, his comment was simply, " Well, lads, some we win, some we lose! But we still have a lot to do." He then contemplated we sorry looking bunch, who only possessed what we stood up in and said, "Follow me lads." At that time we were rather derogatory of the RAF saying, that they could not organise a piss-up in a brewery but as Dan led us into a large EP1 tent we suddenly had to eat our words. There in the middle of a battle zone, hundreds of miles from base, was a fully-fledged clothing store! As we were re-kitted from head to toe and given a couple of blankets each, we had to admit that the organisation was pretty good!

The next location to which we were assigned proved to be much more fruitful. We were despatched in three wagons to El Acroma, situated between Derna and Tobruk. This was the spot from which Mussolini had launched his original assault in 1940 and where he had erected an impressive "Victory" column. The location was obviously quite important to the Italians and was where the LRDG had observed lots of activity as the Axis[13] prepared to construct a radio station. When we eventually found the spot it appeared that the Germans had left in a great hurry and, probably thinking that it was a strategic withdrawal, had left all of the equipment for the new station behind and simply covered it with stones and sand. When we removed the covering we found a huge stash of unopened packing cases, all were

---

13   The name given to the German and Italian forces combined

stencilled with the Afrika Corp insignia and the Wehramacht Signals Corp logo. Unable to believe our good fortune, we got to work with a will. In the region were lines of telegraph poles, erected by the Italians for communication, and with the aid of the toolkits and equipment carried on board our wagons we managed to fell about half a dozen of these poles. We sawed them into convenient lengths and with the aid of ropes and block and tackle; we used them as rollers to load the cases onto our wagons. One particular crate weighed several tons and took a lot of muscle power to load but we were determined to clear the site. I am sure that the Germans must have been flabbergasted when they returned about a month later!

Back at El Aden, Dan and his boffins were delighted and of course at the time, the rest of our lads were busy on similar missions over the entire battlefield. One party who entered Benghazi achieved one particular coup, of which our unit was particularly proud. They "looted" Radio Benghazi, completely stripping it of all its equipment, including the large transmitter and all was spirited away to our base in Egypt. Of course, Dan's orders were to clear up the whole battlefield and get out smartly before Rommel counter-attacked using one of his expert circling movements. On several occasions we saw supply convoys being escorted by the LRDG, not only with their jeeps armed with machine guns, but by huge American Mack & White wagons. These wagons looked like supply trucks but on closer inspection had a 25lb artillery piece mounted on its chassis, covered by a tarpaulin!! What a fighting unit they were!

By the end of January, news began to get through that Rommel had struck again at El Agheila. Very quickly we, together with AAHQ, were ready for withdrawal. We had all learned the art of quick mobile warfare and this time we did not bother with the Diamond Route, instead we all got back via Mussolini's coast road, via Balbia. This of course meant renegotiating Halfaya Pass, on the Egyptian/Libyan frontier. This pass had been christened "Hell Fire Pass" by our forces in the previous battle and it was heavily pitted. By managing to dodge the shell holes our convoy got down fairly smartly and was soon back in Egypt's Western Desert, leaving the Germans to scratch their heads over the beautifully cleared up battlefield and the loss of all radio equipment!

Once clear of the Libyan frontier our convoy quickly trundled eastward. We were told by the C/O that we were heading back to square one near Helwan. Passing Solum, our first night's stop was near Sidi Barrani, day 2 was near Mersa Matruh and so on, until we reached the beautiful city of Alexandria. There, we were all given a few hours leave to visit the great Navy Club with all of it's facilities. First on the agenda was an ice-cold drink followed by a hearty meal and finally the heaven sent luxury of a hot bath! After going without a decent wash for two months you can imagine what a treat that was! We then passed through the Nile Delta to Cairo and beyond to Tura el Asmant, our final destination.

Stan Wainwright and me driving in the Western Desert

One of our wagons just after hitting a mine

View from El Adam of Tobruk Under Fire

*Abandoned Stuka in the Western Desert with
our tent securely anchored down*

*Mussolini's Victory Column El-Acroma Libia
1941, note the Welsh welcome*

Mural painted on the walls of old buildings in Bardia, Libya, by an artist in the 8th Army

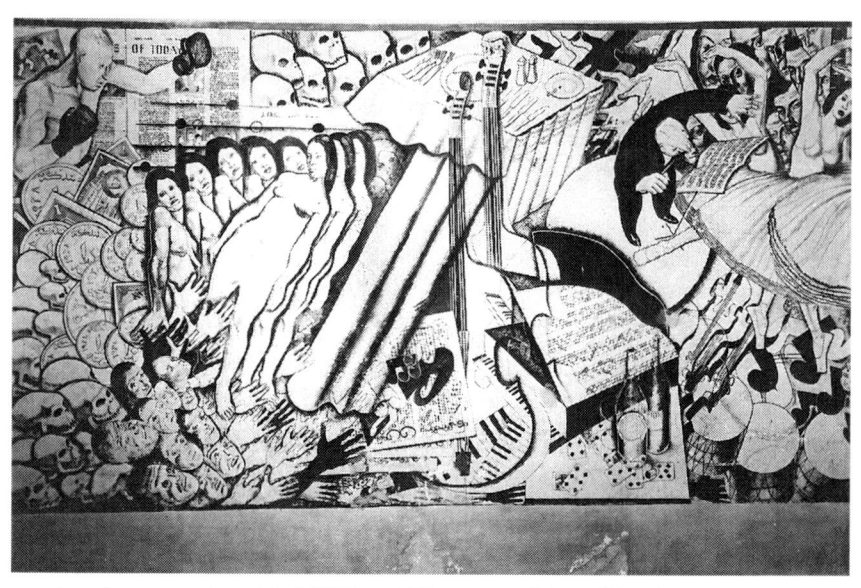

Another mural entitled "Wine, Women and Song" by the same artist.

German dug out in Libya

Me with German Helmet from dugout

Howitza, mounted on French tank chasse, intact and unused, captured in Libya 1941

Captured Italian tanks near El Alimain

Abandoned ME109

Knocked out German 75mm anti-tank gun

Result of Desert Airforce bombing

Result of Desert Airforce bombing

CHAPTER 7

The Caves of Tura, the Clock Goes Back

Over the next twelve months we were to witness the efficiency, which had gone into the building of the RAF. Under strict security, we were to help establish 111 Maintenance Unit and the site chosen lay amongst the quarries in the hills, on the eastern bank of the Nile. These hills were on the same range which houses the Valley of the Kings but much further south in the Kingdom. These hills, at Tura, were riddled with ancient caves, which we were to use as workshops. Most importantly for we lads, was the opportunity to live and breath Ancient Egypt. These caves and their surroundings pre-dated the Pyramids and went back in time for probably some 6000 years; many of the local people we came into contact with lived in conditions that had changed very little.

Mainly Coptic Christians, who were the direct descendants of the Ancient Egyptians, populated the area. These people had converted to Christianity at the time of the Roman occupation and they still used the ancient ways of irrigation and of cultivating the land. They ploughed the land using wooden ploughshares, drawn by oxen and they raised water from one level to another by using counter-balanced leather buckets, camel treadmills and unbelievably, Archimedes Screws.

Many of the vessels we saw on their canals and on the Nile could have belonged to the time of the Pharaohs. The caves allocated to us dated back to the First Dynasty of the Old Kingdom and were on an old ledge some 100ft up in the hills. Lower levels had subsequently been quarried and cleared, ours had been filled with rubble, and the RAF had a mammoth task ahead of them.

Fortunately, there was plenty of local labour available, the Egyptian land owners at that time, paid the fellaheen[14] 3 piaster (3p) a day to work on the land but the RAF were able to offer them the princely sum of 12 piaster (12p) a day. Needless to say everyone flocked to the caves for employment. I can still picture the scene of endless streams of men in white galabeers and balanced on their heads were string baskets filled with the rubble to be used in the forming of a treacherously steep road, stretching from the quarry floor to the ledge 100 ft above. As the caves were cleared out we marveled at the achievement of those ancient people. Here, at Tura, they had found the most perfect milky white limestone in the world, which was perfect for their masons to carve with Bronze Age tools for the construction of temples and statues.

Deep tunneling into the hills to extract this beautiful stone had created the caves and there were dozens of caves in our group, most being at least 30 ft square. They went hundreds of feet into the hills and we could see that the stone had been extracted in 6 ft cubes, the chisel marks on the cave interior seemed as fresh as the day they were made. It humbled us greatly as we contemplated the expertise of those ancient stonemasons and the hard work that must have been involved in the project.

Directly across the Nile from Tura is the site of the first capital of the Old Kingdom, Memphis, and Sakkara it's sacred burial ground. The city had been called Whitewall because a magnificent, high, gleaming white wall surrounded it. Obviously, our caves pre-dated even the ancient capital, of which today there is no evidence. The quarries further along the hills are still very much in use today, they provide the white limestone for a very modern cement works near the village of

---

14   Name given to the Egyptian peasants

Tura, hence the name of our then location, Tura the Cement. As the caves were cleared, this lovely material was used to create smooth floors and to construct a roadway around the ledge and into the caves. For security, each cave was sealed off with massive iron doors and all this in a relatively short time!

One of the caves was delegated to Signals Research Section but our first job was to drive our 18 wagons up this very steep and narrow gradient for unloading. That, I must admit, was one hair-raising experience; there was absolutely no room for error!

The interior of our cave had been whitewashed and illuminated with electric light thanks to a German generator found in the large crate, which we loaded at El Acroma. This cave gave the impression of having at some time in the distant past been used as a burial chamber because there were small tunnels leading off the main one but we did immediately find that our main cave was split into two sections. The innermost area was sealed off with a steel grating and securely locked, in that area, referred to as Station X the boffins worked in secret with all the goodies we had found, the rest of us worked in the front area called Signals Repair Section, we were servicing 1081/2 sets for aircraft and TR9 radio pack sets for the army and over a period we produced many hundreds of those but really we were just a cover up for the important work going on in the background, this was kept deadly secret.

During the first month of our stay at Tura, I made contact with Hubert, sister Eileen's husband, we had always been very close and had worked together at Bees Nurseries when I first left school and of course when he and Eileen got married at the very beginning of the war. I had been their best man so indeed he was like a brother to me. At the outbreak of hostilities, Hubert had joined the Royal Armoured Corp, trained in Dorset and gone out in 1940 with the 11th Hussars to join the 8th Army. They had played a prominent part in Operation Crusader; being the scout cars of the 7th Armoured Division and unknown to me Hubert had been in the first armoured car to enter Bengazi where they had struck a mine, badly injuring the crew. When we first made contact he was still in hospital recuperating and his entire unit was back in reserve at Abysia barracks in Cairo being re-equipped with Rover Armoured cars. Once we got in touch we used to meet regularly in Cairo during his off duty hours. Mostly we met at the YMCA at Exbekia Gardens and here I got to know all of Hubert's comrades. What a fine set of lads they were, nearly all had been recruited in the Caernarfon area and were Welsh speaking.

In their company I learned something of the "cuteness" of our army intelligence, for during the battle in Libya when the Germans, with the help of the Enigma, had the upper hand in communications. These lads, all wireless op gunners, passed on information to the rest of the Armoured Division in Welsh! This confused not only the Germans but also the non-Welsh speakers on our side, I thought it was a brilliant move. Of course when we met at the YMCA those young lads did what all Welshmen do when they get together – they sang! When between 20 and 30 of them assembled and struck up with the Welsh hymn singing everyone in the YMCA was captivated. It used to send a chill down my spine every time I heard them singing that great hymn, Gwahoddiad, It was always one of my favorites.

As I mentioned earlier, many of the Egyptians in the Tura area were not Muslims but Coptic Christians and many of them worked for the YMCA and I recall that on one occasion a particular young man I knew quite well came to see me after listening to them sing and said in Arabic, "Taman Owee" which roughly translated means "Da iawn". To me that said it all, those young lads, although they were there fighting a deadly war, were great ambassadors for peace and although many of them (including Hubert) never returned to their beloved North Wales I feel their legacy still lives on today in our famous International Eisteddfod at Llangollen.

More mention must be made of those amazing ancient caves in which we were establishing the MU, the last of the series, on the edge of the escarpment was the largest of all, thousands of tons of stone must have been extracted from it, the road had been driven through it and exited on the other side of the hills. From that viewpoint, hundreds of feet up and overlooking the Nile Valley, the scene was absolutely breathtaking.

Gazing to the left and south across the Nile you could just discern the group of pyramids at Dashur, this group included the Bent Pyramid and directly below us was the site of ancient Memphis and the sacred burial ground of Sakkara with the famous Stepped Pyramid. This was the oldest stone monument in the world that housed the burial chamber of the Pharoah Djoser (Zoza), he was the first ruler of the United Kingdom of Upper and Lower Egypt and his monument was their first venture into that particular design. Previously they had excavated underground chambers which were covered by a square stone mastaba, but here they experimented by placing a smaller mastaba on the first and so on until eventually they placed a very small one at the top, so achieving a pyramid shape. Following this attempt they went in for extensive pyramid building, many hundreds were erected, probably over a period of 1000 years. The best bent one, at Dasher, was evidence of how they got the angle wrong and changed it half way up and on that site there was also the remains of a pyramid that had collapsed during construction.

Lifting our eyes above Sakkara and the palm fringed Nile bank we could see the vast baked emptiness of the Western Desert and far to our right the city of Cairo and the pyramids of Giza. There the building of the mammoth structures finally reaches perfection. The pyramids of Khufu and Khfra were given a final outer casing of smooth Tura limestone; can you imagine what a sight those gleaming white structures must have been at the time of completion? Sadly they lost their outer casing after the Arab conquest when the beautiful white stone was used to construct much of modern Cairo leaving the pyramids as the rough structures we see today. Upon returning to our caves we noticed that close by one cave in particular had a high wire fence and locked gates surrounding it and was heavily guarded by the Egyptian army. In that cave was housed all the treasures of the Cairo museum, including Tutankarman, all secured against air raids.

There is one final story regarding a cave in our group, which I feel is worthy of mention. During excavation it was found, like the others, to be filled to the roof with rubble but this one proved to be unique because as the workmen began removing the debris they suddenly uncovered the top of a very large hieroglyphic tablet, the only one to be found in the area. With such an important discovery work was stopped immediately and an urgent message was sent to Cairo. As a result, within a short time, a team of Egyptologists arrived and amid great excitement they uncovered part of the panel. They soon ascertained that this had been a temple chamber associated with human sacrifice! As it was late in the day and the fact that they were only able to study the panel by torchlight they decided to recover the whole tablet and return at first light the next day to carry out a detailed survey.

No thought had been given to mounting an armed guard at the cave for the night so can you imagine the horror and dismay for everyone concerned when they turned up the following morning to complete the investigation of this very important find, to discover that during the night the entire hieroglyph had been uncovered and all of the images chiseled off!! After lying undisturbed for 5000 years this valuable piece of information had been removed in a few hours. Who on earth, we wondered, would have done such a thing. Could the Copts, these descendants of ancient Egypt, have been responsible? Maybe, removing information that they did not want the Western world to discover. We do find that on many occasions during Egyptian history there had been turbulence when a dynasty adopted new beliefs and questioned the Old Gods. Sometimes all evidence of a certain ruler would be obliterated in this manner; could something along those lines be responsible for this action? We will never know.

What a privilege it was for we lads to be living among these ancient people, the sheer time scale of Egyptian history made us feel humble indeed. During our short spell at Tura we were determined to grasp every opportunity to explore the area and I feel certain that in doing so we crammed a lifetime of experience into that brief period. We were here in the very cradle of civilization, the area where Egyptian civilization was born. The people who originally settled in the Nile Valley cultivated the fertile land that they found and lived in humble mud brick buildings. Here at Tura as they evolved into the Bronze Age, they developed the art of Stone Masonry, obtaining stone from our quarries and becoming the greatest engineers, architects and artistic masons the world had ever known. The more we studied the subject, the more fascinated we became with the extreme antiquity of everything we encountered. The Old Kingdom, which we were studying, encompassed the first to the fourth dynasties but when the centre of power moved up the Nile Valley to Thebes and Karnak, establishing the New Kingdom, the civilization progressed to the 31st dynasty (about 300BC). When we contemplate that each of these dynasties represented a greater time span than any of the Great Empires that have succeeded it the very thought is mind blowing.

The fortunate thing about our location was that Helwan was linked to Cairo by a very modern rail system. A German contractor had constructed this railway during the 1930's, and GANZ of Budapest made the modern diesel locomotives and rolling stock. Obviously because of this the Germans had a good deal of knowledge of the area. This excellent, fast service took us to Bab el Louk station in Cairo; here I must make comment about this immaculate station. It was constructed entirely of white and yellow glazed bricks, it was a masterpiece and when I made enquiries I was told that the bricks had been made at the Standard Brick Yard in Buckley! What a small world!

By this time of course we were getting to know Cairo like the back of our hand and from there we could board an ancient tramway which took us over the Nile and across Gazera Island to the foot of the Plateau at Giza. It is on this plateau that the Great Pyramids and the Sphinx stand and we spent a great deal of time exploring that area; the great advantage we had was that in those days it was not commercialized. Hubert and his comrades often accompanied me on my visits there. The sheer size of the pyramids was beyond belief; each one covered an area of thirteen acres and from corner to corner was perfectly level. Each one contained more than two million huge sandstone blocks. Even today, in the 21st century, engineers are mystified at how those ancient people accomplished such a massive task. On one of our visits a guide took us inside Khufus' Great pyramid, the guide was armed only with a torch. This was not a visit I would recommend to anybody with a fear of confined spaces! When we finally climbed up to the King's chamber, halfway up the interior, we gazed in disbelief at the size of the granite slabs, which formed the chamber. How on earth, we wondered, could those ancient people have raised these giant stones to this height, altogether they must have weighed many hundreds of tons!

After some three months at Tura I had occasion to get to know the interior of our hospital cave fairly well. I was struck down with Yellow Fever and this disease, we were told, had accounted for the deaths of half of De Leseps work force when they had cut the Suez Canal. Yellow Fever and dysentery had been responsible for 75% of the casualties in the First World War campaign against the Turks. Fortunately for me, by the 1940's medical science had come up with a cure for the Yellow Fever, so consequently I had just a three week stay and as my bed was situated directly beneath the Hieroglyphic panel it was then that I had learned all about that amazing find. One day we had a visit from an old gentleman in a black suit, he came to chat with me, and the lad in the next bed. He proved to be one of the Egyptologists who had come to study the panel. At that time most of the experts in the Cairo museum were British as was this gentleman, and it was he who told me of the heart breaking destruction of the panel. We also learned that some twenty years previously he been involved in tomb exploration in the Valley of the Kings with none other than Howard Carter.

Upon my release from "Dock", the unit decided to give me a short break with light duties; this spell proved to be quite an adventure in itself! A fellow ex-patient (non other than my old pal Sgt Chalky White) and myself were given the job of being armed escort to a convoy of three wagons destined for HQ RAF Levant, which if my memory serves me right was Ramleh. As our consignment consisted of bomb bays, machine guns and ammunition and we were traveling through hostile territory, Chalky and I were armed to the teeth. Boy! Some light duty! For several weeks of our duty we lived and slept rough as we crossed Northern Egypt, skirted the Great Bitter Lake, crossed the Suez Canal (via a rickety old pontoon bridge) and crossed the Sinai Desert to the Promised Land! Having Chalky with us was a godsend, he was a time expired "Old Sweat" who had been in the Middle East since before the war and had volunteered to carry on for the duration. He spoke Arabic like a native and knew every inch of the territory. He was a hive of information, the series of Bitter lakes, he explained, had been linked by De Leseps to form the canal. He then went on to tell us of his theory that the vast Great Bitter Lake, alongside which we camped on our second day, was the scene of the Exodus. Chalky explained that 4000 years ago this spot was a tidal inlet of the Red Sea and that about where we were standing the Israelites had crossed at low tide and the pursuing Egyptian army with their chariots, were caught by the rising waters. When we studied this, his idea seemed to make a lot of sense.

Once over the canal we had the hazardous crossing of the Sinai Desert to encounter; what a godforsaken, barren and desolate place that is! After two hard days and nights we eventually reached the dusty little Arab town of Beershiba and as we trundled through this primitive place, which could have come directly out of the pages of the Old Testament, the hostile stares we received gave us the impression that we were not welcome. We were more than relieved that we were only passing through. I wonder, had those fierce looking tribesmen known what our wagons contained, would they have let us through? We were thankfully soon out of their sight and back in the wide-open desert. Some miles north of Beershiba we came across a small army unit, just three or four huts inside a good secure enclosure. We were made most welcome but as no food was on offer in their mess room we made our own usual arrangement of "brew" and "nosh" under the wagons. This unit had kindly offered us the use of their empty huts as shelter for the night. We were most grateful and duly rolled out our bedding on the floor. During the night we all began to feel rather uneasy and when one of the lads eventually switched on a torch we discovered to our horror that the whole building was "alive" with big, black body bugs, the size of a fingernail! We were being bitten to death! You have never seen such a rapid evacuation. All were frantically shaking bedding, we were indeed glad to spend the rest of the night, as usual, rolled up under our wagons. Needless to say, our departure the next morning was an extremely early one and without any extended thanks to our hosts.

Soon after this incident we arrived at our final destination, HQ Levant and were thankful indeed to be relieved of our precious cargo. We were then free to return to our base at Tura with empty wagons. However, this was where Chalky played his trump card. As senior man of the party and someone who new the Holy Land intimately, he suddenly announced, " Hold it lads, while we are here we might as well have a bit of a holiday". That was precisely what he then proceeded to give us, a guided tour courtesy of HM Government! First he took us over the winding Seven Sisters road, through beautiful orange groves, vineyards etc, to the Holy city of Jerusalem, where we spent two nights at the TocH hostel sleeping between heavenly white sheets.

We were able to take in all the sights of the city, journeying on donkeys down the Kedron Valley, to the Garden of Gethsemone to see the Stone of Agony inside the church there, to the Wells of Siloam and then to ascend the Mount of Olives. Chalky went to great lengths to point out places of interest on the next part of our tour, which was a visit to Bethlehem. Returning to the TOCH that evening, following a very tiring day exploring Jerusalem, I expressed my excitement about our proposed visit to Bethlehem the next day. Imagine my disappointment on discovering that none of the other lads were in the least bit interested; all that they wanted to do was to explore Jerusalem again. My disappointment abated though when Fareed, who ran the hostel, said to me, "Don't worry, I can arrange that for you". Fareed was a very well dressed and well-spoken gentleman who I assumed to be a Coptic Christian. He promised to give me a covering letter to present to his brother who lived in Bethlehem and who, Fareed assured me, would gladly show me around. The arrangements were simplicity itself; all that I had to do was to go to the Jaffa gate and catch the Egged bus at 08.30 the next morning for Bethlehem.

The next morning, appropriately dressed and armed, I made my way to the Jaffa Gate and there I spotted a rickety old bus with no glass in the windows. The word Egged was emblazoned on the front but all other signs were in Arabic and Hebrew. To reassure myself that this was the bus I enquired by saying, "Betlem?" I received nods so I confidently hopped on board. There was not another serviceman in sight and the bus was crowded with Arabs but clutching my covering letter for confidence, I took my seat amongst them. An old Arab gentleman, who had obviously been to market, came to sit alongside me together with his wicker cage containing half a dozen hens.

When we eventually got under way the road to Bethlehem proved very dusty and bumpy, I was so glad of the *open* windows to get some fresh air! The journey seemed to take about an hour and eventually we arrived in the centre of the town. I got off the bus at what looked like the town square and from there soon found Fareed's brother. He was the proprietor of a gift shop and when I introduced myself and gave him the covering letter he was only too pleased to show me around his shop! Commercialism had taken over! I bought a few gifts from him but I was pleased when at last I could make my getaway. Once outside the shop I encountered a small Arab boy who approached me and said, "Guide sir?" I duly gave him the required 10 piatres, which I was to find was worth every penny, the lad proved to be a gem.

He took me into the square where I had left the bus, which proved to be the frontage of the Church of the Nativity. The young boy explained in perfect English, that the Crusaders had built the church. I noticed that the main door had been bricked up leaving just a very small doorway and you had to bend to gain access. The reason for this was that the church had changed hands many times during the wars and this alteration was to prevent the Turks from entering the church on their camels and horses and using the church as stabling. Once inside the church the young lad pointed out the Altar of the Innocents, built by the Crusaders to commemorate Herod's act of killing all male babies. We then went into a crypt, in a cave beneath the church. In there was a ledge where he explained was the alleged spot where Christ had been born. I spent some considerable time in that wonderful place.

Eventually I went out into the sunshine to say farewell and thank you to the young lad. It had been such a wonderful experience for me and that youngster, who probably did not go to school, had proved such a knowledgeable and informative guide. It made me feel quite humble to think that having had no formal education, this young lad had gained so much knowledge about the holy places and had obtained an excellent command of the English language. I on the other hand had had the advantage of a Secondary Education but my familiarity of Arabic was very rudimentary indeed. I have often wondered what became of that young lad, especially when you consider the troubled times that followed.

I returned to the TocH hostel in Jerusalem having had one of the most wonderful days of the *holiday*. For our final visit, Chalky took us across the plains of Jezreel to Nazereth. As a youngster, just a few years prior to this time, I had heard all about these places in Sunday school and I had to pinch myself to realize what I was seeing. Finally, our holiday over, we retraced our steps across Sinai, this time carefully avoiding that "hospitable" little army camp! We were soon back over the canal and back at our home base, Tura. The spell of convalescence had certainly worked wonders with Chalky and I, and any effect of our confinement in hospital had long worn off. So now it was back again to cave duty. By now we "Front Lads" were turning out a great volume of reconditioned radio equipment but there was never any doubt in our minds that the real vital work was going on in our cave's interior by the "secret men" who rarely showed their faces. This was evident by the constant stream of VIP military leaders who called. Our most regular and almost daily visitor was Air Chief Marshall Teddar, AOC in C.M.E. (Air Officer Commander in Chief, Middle East) and another frequent visitor was the most high ranking RAF officer, Marshall of the RAF "Boom" Trenchard; you can't go higher than that!

The most memorable of visitors was, I think, in July or August 1942. We were instructed one day to "put on your very best KD tomorrow, lads, we are expecting a very special visitor". Next morning we all turned out "spick and span" as instructed and as we lined up in front of our cave we saw in the distance a battered old staff car struggling up out treacherous, narrow cliff roadway. When it finally made it to our cave entrance can you imagine our joy when out of the car popped a portly figure, clad in a blue siren suit, topi on his head and a large cigar in his mouth, it was Winston Churchill himself! The Top Brass of all three services, which included Field Marshall Alan Brook (C.I.G.S.), accompanied the great man but as "Winnie" leapt out and dashed through our cave to the inner sanctuary, none of his entourage were agile enough to keep up with him. As he emerged once again into the bright sunlight, Winnie's face was a picture, leaving us in no doubt at all that during our lightening strike on Libya we had uncovered something of great importance. Possibly this was the final piece of the jigsaw in the colossal fight to break the German strangle hold with the ENIGMA. It was then, in great mood, that Winnie found an old ammo box to stand on and told us all to gather round. As we did so, in parade ground order, he shouted, "Sit down lads, so that I can see your faces". I recall thinking to myself at the time how Jock would have loved that moment.

What followed was probably the highlight of my wartime service, the one point which made it all worthwhile because Mr Winston Churchill addressed we few dozen lads with our very own version of one of his famous wartime speeches which had been the rallying cry to the nation. Firstly, he introduced us to all the Service Chiefs, including General Montgomery, who had just come out from Blighty with him to take over the Eighth Army. We all knew that General Gott, commander of the 7th Armoured was in line to take over but he had, tragically, been killed in an air crash. I remember Mr Churchill making one introduction which I felt was a little off the mark. Among the party was the American Ambassador to Britain, Mr Avril Harriman and as Winston presented him to us he said, "Gentlemen, the future President of the United States". I think that was one prediction Mr Churchill did not get quite right! We all felt really proud as he thanked us for the contribution we were making and told us that everything was in hand for the forthcoming Battle of El Alamain. His parting shot was, "And now lads, together we are going to make the final push and throw the Nazi Hun and his Italian lackey out of North Africa". With that they all loaded into the old staff car and were off in a cloud of dust. As they were leaving the site and heading towards our Big cave, which we called the cathedral, we all gave chase. At the end of the cave they all got out to admire the view of the Nile Valley and it was at this point that Winnie threw away his cigar butt. One of the lads was lucky enough to retrieve it as a souvenir (and what a valuable one it was) and who knows, maybe today it will be proudly displayed in some family china cabinet! Before they climbed back into the staff car, I heard Winston say. "Gaze on ye mighty and despair", he was of course quoting Pharaoh Rameses II when he was referring to his monuments and statues.

Prior to Churchill's visit, we troops behind the lines had been quite perturbed by reports of the reinforcement of German and Italian troops at Alemain. They were right on the doorstep of Egypt and it was thought likely that they would occupy Alexandria at any time. Rumour had it that they were planning their victory march through Cairo, which would have been led by the German Panzer divisions accompanied by Mussolini leading his Italian legions upon white horse! Fortunately the reinforcements did not amount to the number that Rommel had wanted to allow him to capture the Persian oilfields and link up with the Russian front. Although subsequent opinions were that Hitler had made a big mistake in not supplying sufficient power to his pincer movement, it is possible that his military resources were fully stretched and he was unable to do so. At the same time our armies were able to gain strength with the introduction of the American Sherman 30 ton tank, the equal of the Panzer Mark 4. The Mark 4 had previously been invincible against our Valentine light armoured tanks and had knocked them out at will.

Now vast numbers of artillery regiments were flooding in and following Aukinlec's first battle at El Alamain a firm line of defence had been established when he had halted the German army forcing them to dig in. There followed much kidology regarding the position of our defences, was it to the south, at the edge of the Qattara Depression or was it the northern Med. Side? Eventually a massive array of artillery opened up simultaneously covering the entire front creating the greatest bombardment ever. This lasted some fifteen minutes and so shocked the Germans that their defences were reeling. However, they held firm and the battle lasted for some days before they eventually cracked and allowed a break through that finally became a headlong retreat.

Now in our cave dwelling we still maintained a contact with the LRDG. Those great warriors of desert warfare used to call on us whenever they had trouble with the radio equipment in their fighting vehicles. No red tape existed between us; we would just fix the problem and see them on their way. Following the battle of El Alamain and when we had fulfilled our task at 111 M.U., most of us were transferred back to mobile units in Libya for the next phase of operations but before we move onto that stage I think that our final exploration in the Nile Valley, which did indeed prove to be very memorable, is worth relating.

Our unit Padre had for a long time been organizing weekly study groups, which most of us attended, the object being to discover as much as possible about local history and archaeology.

He impressed us lads very much with his theories of what had occurred on the spot that we occupied. Here, he suggested, the Israelites had been held in bondage, working on the building of the pyramids. Our caves were the ones suggested by Joseph, the advisor to Pharaoh, for the storage of grain to feed the nation during the Great Plague and Famine, which he predicted, would occur. To further our study, when we were all off duty, the Padre arranged a weekend outing to cross the Nile and journey by camel and donkey to Memphis and Sakkara. To facilitate this he had established the help of our unit Bash Ries[15], a local man named Raatib, he was a Coptic Christian who was in charge of all Egyptian labour on the unit, he had plenty of connections and was a good organizer. We were a party of about fifty and it was the responsibility of each man to ensure that he carried sufficient rations and water for the outing. No transport was provided, so the first stage of the expedition was a long trudge from our camp of several miles across the desert to the ancient jetties on the banks of the Nile at Tura. These jetties were probably the same ones, or at least on the same site, used by the ancient Egyptians to carry the white Tura limestone to Memphis and the Pyramids at Giza. There we found a vessel tied up and ready for our river crossing. It was a vessel which could well have come from that period, it was a huge flat-bottomed Felucca, especially built for stone carrying. For propulsion it relied entirely on a massive single triangular sail, this showed its age by being well and truly patched!

---

15   The title given to the leader of the local labour force

When we were all eventually safely embarked on the felucca, it became apparent that this was no luxury cruise. The entire bottom of the vessel was deeply covered in limestone rubble, which was obviously the chippings left behind from cargoes over goodness knows how many years. We simply had to stand in a huge group right across the vessel with the lucky ones sitting in the gunwales. After a good deal of strenuous poling we were in deep enough water to hoist the great sail and we set off upstream. The Nile at this point, was quite wide, probably half a mile or more and we had to proceed a considerable distance before reaching a navigable point where it was possible to cross over to the small "modern" village of Hedema. This village was on the site of the great capital of the Old Kingdom and as we approached, the large sail still full of wind, the vessel came in "beam on" and we beached in a spot that was obviously regularly used as the bank at that spot was liberally covered with limestone chippings. From what we could ascertain, the village comprised of a series of wattle and daub huts. The people occupying the site must have led a fairly primitive existence but as we arrived they all turned out to greet us. A great mass of people (all male) dressed in white galabeers had assembled a great parade of camels and donkeys, sufficient for all of us to ride on our exploration. After some discussion we were informed that Sakkara was a good distance away and the journey would entail many hours of hard riding. We began to have doubts regarding the wisdom of our planned day out, thinking that we had probably been rather optimistic.

Eventually we all began to mount the animals of our choice. My choice was a camel for which I had been supplied a stone carrying wooden frame to substitute for a saddle; not the most comfortable ride! We duly set of on the first stage of our exploration. To escort us the village band had turned out and this caused some amusement amongst the lads. All the band members played some kind of homemade flute cut from bamboo. The band, was of course, accompanied by the usual big drum to keep time but the whole effect, to our Western ears, was a rhythmic wailing sound rather than musical accompaniment. We followed a well-beaten track through the palm and eucalyptus groves, the whole area covered in lush vegetation, very different to the opposite bank that we had just left.

Eventually we reached an area, which was littered with ancient remains. This seemed to be the site of a Palace or Temple as among the undergrowth we found many small sphinxes and among the palm trees many fallen statues of the mighty pharaohs. Everything was very overgrown and so after some exploration we decided that as this was quite a cool spot and well shaded from the hot sun by the palm trees, we would take a break and consume some of our rations. It was at this point that our leader, the Padre, came around to tell us that things did not seem to be going according to plan; trouble seemed to be brewing! A fierce argument appeared to be going on between the village elders and Raatib our guide. In the normal course of events we were quite used to this sort of thing as among the Egyptians threatening behavior and shouting was simply their way of making conversation and all usually ended in a friendly way. In this case however, the row had soon developed into violence and of course due to our limited knowledge of Arabic, we had no idea what it was all about.

Maybe not enough backsheesh[16] was forthcoming, or could it be that Raatib had reneged on the price agreed for our mode of transport? We had no idea. As things looked rather threatening the Padre decided that we must cut short our visit and get back to the safety of the felucca as soon as possible. As we began to make a hasty retreat, we all noticed that the crowds, which now surrounded us, had multiplied dramatically and had grown very hostile, so much so that we had to dodge the occasional missile! One pessimist amongst us suggested that the boatmen were in on the conspiracy and had sailed off without us, in which case we were trapped! Fortunately, as we approached the river, we could see our vessel, still beached and waiting for us with gangplanks down. As we abandoned our animals and made a dash for safety, we found that hundreds more angry people had gathered on the bank overlooking our boat. We suddenly came under fire as heavy hails of rocks were thrown at us by the mob. Now we knew their intention and realizing that we were unarmed they would certainly close in on us to stone us to death. Thankfully, luck was on our side, remember ours was a stone carrying boat, the bottom deep in limestone rubble, just what was needed at that moment. As the mob advanced, subjecting us

---

16   Back-hander or tip

to a constant barrage of rocks, we crouched behind the gunwales for shelter. Just at the right time the Padre fearlessly stood on the prow and judging his moment he suddenly shouted, "Right lads, Fire". At that we let go a heavy salvo and as we kept up the bombardment the crowd quickly withdrew, out of range.

As the medics among us began patching up the wounded, a sudden cry went up, "Where is Raatib?" We looked back to the riverbank to see him surrounded by the angry mob, being beaten, his life in danger. Like lightening, our brave Padre said, "Quick lads, half a dozen volunteers" and as the rest of us gave covering fire they dashed among the mob grabbing the poor unfortunate Bash Ries and carried him back on board to safety.

Despite all being safely aboard we were certainly not out of the mire yet. Our felucca was well and truly beached, so keeping a constant hail of rocks and rubble aimed at the wild mob, we all bent to with a will, to pole our boat off the bank. Eventually we all breathed a sigh of relief as we drifted clear of our tormentors and hoisted the sail. Our medics patched up poor old Raatib, who had been badly injured but I am glad to say that he did make a full recovery. At the end of a very eventful day, as we sailed quietly back downstream towards Tura, the far bank clad in its palm trees looked so idealistic and peaceful – such vistas can sometimes be very misleading!

RAF Maintence & Research Tura 1941, the caves in the background

Felaheen cultivating the land at Tura

Drawing water using Archemedes Screws

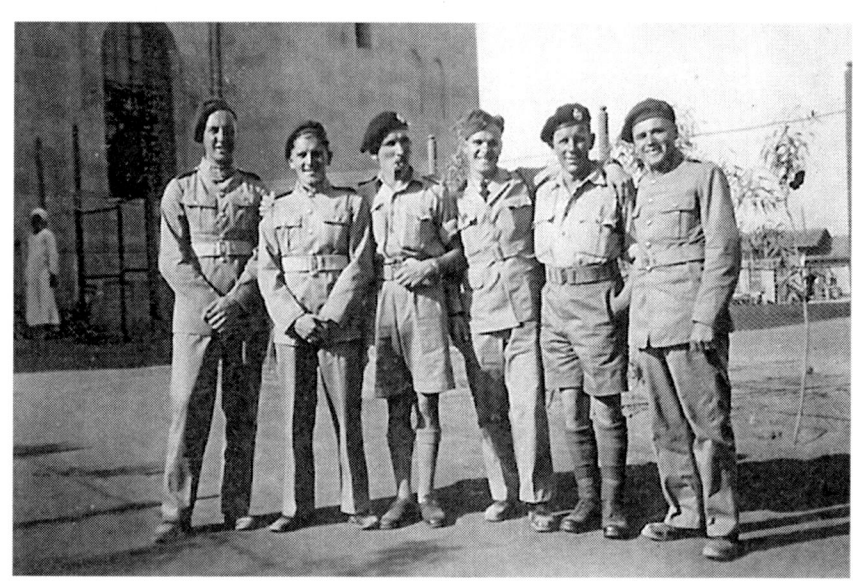

Me (in RAF uniform) with mates from the 7th Armoured Division

My brother in Law Hubert with his Rover Armoured Car

Me & Hubert on the Pyramids at Giza in 1942

Climbing the Great Pyramid 1941

Me on Light duties in Sinia 1942

Cheops Pyramid Giza

Donkey riding in Jerusalem

Young Guides in bethlehem

Entrance to the Church of the Nativity in Bethlehem

Raatib, our guide at Memphis

Boarding a Falucca on the Nile at Tura 1942

Falucas loaded with stone from the Quarry

Me traveling up the Nile

Faluca with a typical patched sail

Our landing place at Memphis, later to be the scene of our stoning

Fallen Statue of Ramisis II at Memphis

Chapter 8

Back up the Blue

Following the victory at El Alemein and the conclusion of our SSU duties at Tura, we lads were again earmarked for duties Up the Blue. This term, Up the Blue, was constantly used during the campaign in the Middle East to indicate Libya and areas west of Egypt and stemmed from passed military activity, probably from as far back as the days of Nelson. However, that is where we were again destined to serve. On posting back to the Desert Air Force we were to form 219 Mobile Signals Unit, this was to be the communication section for 235 Wing, which in turn was just part of 201 Naval Cooperation Group. This group was responsible for Coastal Command Eastern Med., so we were maintaining our tradition of being a small intimate group of wireless operators.

Our wing was not to advance on Tunisia in support of the 8th Army but to operate from Libya, giving air support to their supply convoys and carrying out constant strikes against enemy shipping in the Aegean. Our base was Gambut Main, a flat area on the top of the escarpment, similar to El Adem but situated between Tobruk and Bardea. It was some twenty miles inland and from its very commanding position it was an ideal spot for carrying out our particular operations. Initially, our aircraft operated from makeshift runways, just sand strips, cleared of obstacles by bulldozer, this meant of course that they were extremely dusty and proved to be a nightmare for the aircrafts engine fitters. We were now to witness a miracle of engineering with the arrival of a South African Army Engineers Regiment. They were equipped with huge earth moving machines, stone crushing and grading machines and road rollers. Within a couple of weeks they provided us with an excellent stone runway.

235 Wing consisted of five squadrons, two of which were 252 and 603 both RAF Beanfighters. These wonderfully versatile aircraft armed with 20mm cannons and rockets, a new development, and some armed with torpedoes. These squadrons were the pride and joy of 235 Wing and it was they who carried out very effective strikes against enemy shipping; we understood that the enemy referred to them as "Whispering Death". The remaining three squadrons comprised two RAAF (Royal Australian Air Force) numbers 454 and 459, and one SAAF (South African Air Force) squadron, whose number I cannot recall. These were all equipped with American Hudson and Maryland bombers and were responsible for aerial cover for the convoys carrying 8th Army supplies and voyages to the beleaguered Malta.

The first job for us when we arrived at the site was to provide our own accommodation. The usual idea was to dig a hole, over which you erected your bivouac; this made a nice cool billet. However, my good friend LAC Fred Beeston, from Hull, and I decided on a "Better Ole". We acquired a wrecked Italian Army wagon and with the help of some tarpaulins and a bit of ingenuity, we managed to convert our prize into quite a comfortable little home from home. Some months previous, Gambut had been the spot chosen by Rommel for his headquarters but I doubt whether the old Desert Fox had a more comfortable boudoir than Fred and I. Our mobile unit consisted of large Crosley wagons and trailers. The Crosley housed a large 1085 transmitter and the trailer could accommodate four operators on 1084 receivers. This was quite powerful equipment and gave us a long range. We were later to discover that our role at this particular phase of the war was a dual purpose one.

The first episode that I wish to recall however does not relate to our military activity at Gambut but rather to a memorable day when a group of us stumbled across some ancient remains. Our appetite had been wetted by the many things we had seen in the Nile Delta and when exploring the escarpment. We had a feeling that many of the caves we encountered were not quite natural and we explained this to our C/O and asked his permission for six of us to have a day of exploration to see if we could come up with anything.

He willingly agreed to our request but with some very strict orders:

1. We must all be armed, as the Libyan Sennusi Bedouins were a very wild people
2. We must take with us sufficient rations, including water
3. The rest of the unit must be made aware of which direction we were intending to go

So, thus prepared, we set off at first light the next day and headed East along the top of the escarpment. As we walked, one of the lads who had an interest in geology explained that the high ground that we were following ran parallel to the sea but was some 20 miles inland. He explained that this had in fact, in pre-historic times, been the shoreline when the sea levels were much higher than today. When looking towards the Med., the flat desert below us, had once been the seabed and the much higher Sahara desert behind us had been a very fertile and well populated area, fed by many rivers. The wadis, which we frequently crossed, were in fact the ancient river courses and positioned where they would have entered the sea.

Being young and fit, we followed the top of the ridge for several hours, how far we travelled I could not ever guess but at about midday we came to a rather distinctive area. This was a wadi with a particularly wide mouth and here the escarpment on one side, extended in a large, flat, semi-circular shape and it commanded a panoramic view of the desert below. On close examination we could trace the foundations of many buildings and the large semi-circle seemed to be encompassed by a wall. From this, several cobbled roads seemed to converge on one large building and we came to the conclusion that we had discovered the remains of a Roman Fortress. Our belief was further reinforced with the amazing discovery of what appeared to be two very deep wells that had been formed by cutting through the solid rock. We experimented by throwing stones into the wells, which proved them to be very deep but dry shafts!

We had no means of going down these shafts but as we looked around that amazing site we all agreed that the Romans must have been astounding engineers. In this very arid area they would not have cut out these wells without knowing that there was water below, and then the thought occurred to us that they would have used the stone extracted to build the fort. What we had found was probably a staging post on their long line of communication during the occupation of Egypt. No doubt their highway ran along the top of the ridge we had just followed. We stayed at our find for some considerable time and consumed the rations that we had with us, as I am sure many a Roman soldier had done some two thousand years ago. When we finally made it back to our unit it was almost nightfall, everyone was relieved to see us as they were ready to dispatch a search party. When we recounted our amazing find however the response seemed to be cool, nobody seemed very interested and I cannot recall our find ever being mentioned again and certainly nobody else went out to investigate!

During the following lengthy period of service at Gambut we were of course to experience the desert in its many moods. Unbearable hot days, bitterly cold nights but the worst torment of all was the constant sand storms from which there was no escape. When they blew up you simply had to lie down, cover up and wait for the storm to blow over. We also experienced, as in the previous year, periods of torrential rain, when the desert would be turned into a morass but miraculously following these periods, the whole desert would spring into life. Vast areas would be covered in exotic flowers of every colour and description; this was especially so in the many wadis where streams would appear and the flowers would become more abundant. We always used to wonder how on earth the seeds survived in such a harsh environment, and how old were they? Could they possibly be from the time of a fertile Sahara, so many millions of years ago? Had we had a botanist with us some of these questions could have been answered.

For the next six months, in addition to controlling all aircraft of our wing, our signals unit were involved in one of Churchill's great bluffs in misleading the enemy regarding the invasion of mainland Europe. Being well aware that the Germans were monitoring all of our transmissions and deciphering our codes, we now changed from RAF X code to International Q to give the impression that the Americans were involved. We also masqueraded as Army HQ and were constantly exchanging messages with Base all of which contained misinformation regarding supplies and troop movements. To add to the illusion, hundreds of dummy landing craft were assembled along the coast and daily smoke screens were lit to cover Bengazi and Tobruk harbours. The Germans regularly sent over high-flying reconnaissance aircraft and no doubt, from 30,000 feet all that they saw must have looked very realistic. The whole objective was of course to keep German units locked up in Greece and the Balkans, well away from Italy where the real landings were to be made. We were of course creating the impression that, as the 8th Army pursued Rommel, the 9th Army had moved in to assemble for the invasion. However, the units that did move in were specialist camouflage units who were doing just the opposite and creating fake army camps and landing grounds, all covered in hundreds of dummy, inflatable tanks, guns, aircraft etc. As wireless operators, we were continually improving our skills and trusted that we were leading the Germans a merry dance.

They do say that necessity is the mother of invention, and so it was, with us living in such a harsh environment. It was amazing how many ingenious devices were adapted to make life easier. The one thing that we had in abundance was empty petrol tins and these were put to good use, filled with sand they made excellent walls for the dugouts. They also came into their own being used to make filtration plants, as water was strictly rationed. The tins were mounted one on top of another, the top tin having holes in the bottom and filled with sand, into that we emptied our dirty (grey) water, the liquid then filtered through the sand, through the holes and into the tin below, giving us water suitable for washing and showering. Another ingenious device made of two petrol tins was a common site in all camps, namely the "Desert Lily". This was a cleverly constructed urinal! Probably the most ingenious device of all though was the oil and water furnace used for heating our ovens; these were made of oil drums. The Unit Cooks did do their very best to provide decent food with the rations available but a group of us decided that a spot of "home cooking" was what we really needed so we built our own mini oil/water oven.

We had a regular supply of fresh chicken and eggs, which we obtained from the Senussi by barter; they loved our free issue of cigarettes (V's). The lads always referred to them as "coffin nails" and said that they tasted like dried sawdust but the Beduins enjoyed them so we always had a steady supply of chicken and eggs for an evening "nosh-up". The only let-down was that our chips had to be made with Yams, or Sweet Potatoes as we know them, these were supplied in great quantity from the Nile Delta, but they were not quite to our taste. On one occasion our lads did a bit of scouting around the Officers Mess cookhouse, the unit was well dispersed and the Officers Mess was about half a mile along the escarpment. They found that the mess tent and cookhouse were surrounded by a ring of vehicles, but stacked against one supply wagon they discovered a load of English potatoes; what a find! It was therefore arranged that each evening, after sunset, we would take it in turns to visit our more privileged friends and "borrow" a battledress top full of selected English spuds! We really did begin to enjoy our nightly feast of chicken, egg and chips, just like we remembered back home. However, not every *night raid* went without a hitch. I can still vividly recall with amusement, one night in particular when it was my turn to do the supply run. I set out as normal, armed with a torch and jack-knife, the former to pick my way across the wadi separating us from the Officers Mess, the latter to cut the sack containing the *booty*. All was well as I stealthily entered the compound and the reassuring sound of singing and merriment drifted from the well-lit mess tent (they had electric lighting supplied by mobile generators, we had hurricane lamps!). I proceeded to open a sack and started to select and stow *chippers* into my battle dress top.

Suddenly the mess tent flap was thrown open and the whole area flooded with light! I quickly dived under a nearby water bowser and behind a wheel; I crouched there breathlessly, hoping that I had not been spotted. The officer who emerged was none other than the Unit Administration officer; this man was not very popular with anyone and had the reputation of being a blustering old windbag and, if I were to be caught he would apply his "guts for garters" principle. Fortunately for me, he was rather under the influence and having come out from a well-lit tent, he had not noticed me. But I then discovered why the old windbag had come outside; following a round of the "Trumpet Voluntary", he came over to the spot where I was hiding. Now anyone having served in our forces knows that when in active service, it is quite in order to relieve yourself against the wheel of a wagon! This is just what this officer had in mind but the intended wheel just happened to be the one I was crouched behind! It was at this time that I discovered his liking for Stella beer as he deposited about two pints of the recycled stuff all over me, I was in no position to cry out in protest! When the dirty deed was over and he returned to make merry with his fellow officers, I completed my task and quickly returned with the loot. Can you imagine the screams of laughter I faced when I recounted the events to the lads? It took me a long time to live it down but it was never mentioned outside of our little circle, as to do so would have brought a good thing to an end! Having deposited the spuds with our duty cook, I quickly stripped off and washed down using our filtered water. I must add though, our chicken and chips supper that night, never tasted as good!

On a more serious note, at about this time we suffered a very tragic loss when both our signals officer and adjutant were killed in a flying accident at Tobruk. Their loss of life was entirely due to the great deception game that we were playing. Our wing was equipped with a Walrus[17], with this we could liaise with the air/sea rescue units who covered all our flights; the Walrus could land alongside the launches. The Walrus regularly visited Tobruk for this purpose and it was on one of these flights that the accident occurred. As the aircraft approached to land in the harbour, because of the smoke screen, they fouled a barrage

---

17   Amphibious aircraft

balloon cable and crashed, killing all the crew. It was an extremely sad episode and one that I will never forget as, along with Taff Owen[18], one of our MT drivers I was detailed for the burial party. Our first task was to collect the bodies from the field hospital in Tobruk and then proceed to El Acroma where our two officers were to be buried near to Mussolini's Victory Column, the spot of our previous remarkable find!

It was also at about this time that I was involved, together with a fellow wireless operator, LAC Fred Yates, in an operation which had a traumatic effect on myself, and the remainder of my wartime service and which signalled the end of my spell with the mobile desert unit. Having not kept a diary at that period of the war and although the events I recall are very clear in my mind, even 64 years on, the exact date of this event eludes me; I can only say about mid 1943. On this occasion we were on middle watch (8pm – 8am) and as soon as we took over we found ourselves responsible for the air cover and protection of a supply convoy heading west. I was on the frequency controlling our aircraft and in this instance was 459 Squadron Australian Air Force, Fred was on the naval wavelength. Throughout the night we kept a fairly routine contact, but suddenly, in the early hours and at first light, I received an O.A.[19] call from the escorting aircraft; he had sighted a U boat lying on the bottom, in the direct path of the convoy. It was normal procedure for escorting vessels, to keep a constant listening watch on our aircraft frequencies but for security reasons and to maintain strict w/t silence they could only transmit in an emergency. Immediately, upon receiving the signal I called the responsible escort vessel with the URGENT signal but got no reply, I tried several times but still no response; the convoy was in deadly peril!

On the air, sheer pandemonium now broke out, our HQ at Alex, the main control station, and other units along the coast joined in, but still silence from the convoy. By this time, news had got around our unit and most of the officers, including Group Captain Collins, our wing C/O, had assembled outside our signals trailer as I continued

---

| 18 | Taff came from Oakenholt |
| 19 | O.A. = Highest possible priority |

to signal OA to the convoy. Just as everyone was beginning to feel it was hopeless my mate Fred said, "Call them again, I think they are answering on my frequency". So it turned out, whether by accident or by design, the destroyer wireless operator was receiving on one frequency and transmitting on another! It was just a pure fluke that Fred had picked up the signal. I now transmitted the full details of the sighting and the exact position of the enemy vessel, the full message was then acknowledged via Fred's channel. The convoy must have taken immediate action because, within half an hour they informed us that the U boat had been sunk with depth charges, wreckage and oil had been observed on the surface. Our signals officer, Flight Lieutenant Read, shouted the news across to Groupy, and he instantaneously led all the assembled lads in a rousing cheer.

As Fred and I came wearily off duty, Groupy said, "Come with me lads" and he led us into his tent. There he made out a full report of the entire operation, which he was sending in a despatch. As well as getting an M.I.D. award, he was recommending that we get immediate promotion and the appropriate decoration. Finally, he shook us by the hand, gave us a large tot of whisky and said; "Now lads, go and get some sleep". Our units joy was short lived. A couple of hours later we were rudely awakened and told to quickly report back to the Groupies tent. There we were greeted by a very sombre looking C/O, who informed us that subject to the Official Secrets Act, we were never to mention this event. WE HAD SUNK ONE OF OUR OWN SUBMARINES. Imagine the devastating effect this had, it seemed a complete blanket of silence must be drawn, otherwise heads would roll in high places. I have always kept faith with my promise but feel that after such a lapse of time, the heads that would have rolled have long been laid to rest and I can now speculate on what **I** think **really** happened on that dreadful night.

It has always been my considered opinion that the outcome of our action on that fateful night was and has been ever since, one of those events which occur during a time of war, known as cock-ups and this was a big one. Today this would be referred to as *friendly fire* but there was nothing friendly about it for those on the receiving end. If we read any of the official accounts of the Naval War in the Mediterranean at this period, we will find that the submarine HMS Thunderbolt was sunk by depth charges launched from an Italian Corvette!

I would suggest that the Italian navy was not very active at that time and that Thunderbolt was in fact the vessel involved in our tragic operation. It would be a great relief to me if I were contradicted but nowhere can I find a statement that a mistake was made. The point that weighed heavily on Fred and I was that if he had not intercepted that transmission from the destroyer and I had not then forwarded details of the submarines position, the convoy would in fact have passed safely over the vessel and the lives of her crew would have been safe.

From my point of view, what made the whole episode more poignant was that Thunderbolt was formerly HMS Thetis. That unlucky vessel which was built at Camel Laird, Birkenhead in 1938 had sunk in Liverpool Bay during her first sea trials with the loss of all hands. Many of us will recall how she was recovered from the seabed by an ingenious method using the rise and fall of the tide. Following the gruesome job of salvage and refitting she was re-commissioned as Thunderbolt for war service. Even more moving for me was the fact that an ex-service colleague of mine, Frank Parry from Buckley, a naval man, had actually served on Thunderbolt in the Mediterranean so he obviously would have lost many shipmates. The events of those far off days hang heavily on my shoulders.

Following those catastrophic events our new Signals Officer, the previously mentioned Flight Lieutenant Reid proved himself to be a very able and understanding commanding officer. His first move was to grant Fred and I a fortnights leave in Alexandria. We were to travel from El Adem by the desert "leave train" and this unique journey in itself is worth recording mainly because of the tremendous achievement of our army engineers in constructing the railway. It covered over 500 hundred miles through such hostile territory but what a vital supply line it proved to be, it was operated by a New Zealand army engineer unit.

The journey to Alex was to be a tiring two-day trip through the unbearable desert heat. The carriages had no glass in the windows but instead had shutters to be closed in the event of a sand storm. When the shutters were opened the movement of the train created a wonderful fresh breeze. There were no compartments in the carriages just tables and bench seats for six men every few yards. The train was a weekly affair and the railhead at El Adem was a huge supply depot and transit camp. When the train finally arrived we were all told to board and we found ourselves amongst a good mixture of characters of different nationalities, what good company they all proved to be. One group of six were real rough diamonds of the Green Howards, another a group of New Zealanders and a third group were South Africans. We were a mixed bag all right!

At the very outset of the journey the thing that struck us was the far superior rations issued to the Colonial troops. Our mouths watered as we saw them tucking into tins of ready cooked bacon followed by rice pudding or fruit. We had to be content with our bully and hard tack[20]. Whether they noticed our poor fare I don't know but we all got on well together. At least we were able to supplement our diet with hard-boiled eggs and bread that the enterprising Bedouin had for sale at every halt we came to. These halts were for picking up more troops but these jovial, noisy nomads to whom the train must have been a godsend always surrounded the train.

In addition to the usual eggs and bread, they would conjure up all kinds of things to sell. They were the original "wide boys" and by comparison Del Boy is just a novice.

At one particular stop, Fred and I were conned by a bright Bedouin lad. As the train ground to a halt he ran up alongside and holding up a bag shouted, "Hard boiled eggis, George, six for two piastres". As soon as we completed the transaction he was off like a whippet. This was before we had chance to pelt him with them because on cracking the eggs we found that they were raw. Of course they were of no use to us as we had no means of cooking them on board the train. However, the real smart

---

20   Corned beef and hard biscuits

Just A Tick

guys were the ones who managed to slip aboard and hide themselves until the train was underway. They would them make a quick sale and drop off again, they were taking a big risk as it was strictly a troop train. Locals were forbidden to travel on the train and to enforce this rule the Egyptian authorities provided a police constable guard who constantly patrolled the train from end to end. We witnessed the rough justice he administered to anyone he caught. Without ceremony he would grab them by the scruff of the neck and regardless of how fast the train was travelling, he would throw them off! Those Bedouin must have been as hard as old boots because this seemed to be a regular feature that they took in their stride.

One rather hilarious incident I recall, concerned one such visitor who suddenly appeared in our carriage. Once he knew the coast was clear he emerged and with a handsome flashing smile announced, "Watches, George" as he produced from beneath his flowing galabeer a large card full of shining wristwatches. We of course knew that the street urchins of Alex and Cairo sourced them. These kids were referred to as "Clifty Wallahs" and their speciality was lifting anything of value from the troops. This very smooth salesman made a few *captures* with the New Zealand lads, who seemed a bit flusher than the rest of us.

However by the time he reached our part of the carriage he encountered a group even harder than his people, the Green Howards!

On his sales pitch, "Watches, George", he was greeted with open arms and all six of them tried on his watches in a leisurely fashion. When completely satisfied the corporal, who seemed to be their chief troubleshooter, shouted, "Right lads, heave ho!". At this, they grabbed poor Abdul by his arms and legs, laid him on the table between them and with the train travelling at about 40mph, threw him out of the window. As he left our company he shouted what sounded like "Aneek abook"! Abu is Arabic for father, so I think what he shouted, roughly translated, may have been, "None of you guys knows who your father is"!

As we looked back from the speeding train we saw of our travelling salesman rolling down an embankment in a cloud of dust, picking himself up and waving his fist after the train. No doubt this was all in a days work and he would wander back to his Bedouin tent to prepare another display ready for the next train. Meanwhile, back in the carriage, the smiling Green Howards generously distributed the free watches among the passengers. Things were quiet and back to normal by the time the Egyptian guard returned on his round of inspection.

Maybe these incidents will seem rather cruel and look perhaps like we were taking advantage of people less privileged but this never seemed to be an issue as we all got on well together. There was always plenty of give and take between troops and locals. We were very lucky in that, due to wartime restrictions, general media were banned from theatres of war. The only people allowed were the war correspondents and their reports were subject to military censorship. Perhaps much of the racial hatred evident today is fuelled by the close media scrutiny given to the most minor event just to make news!

Following our spot of leave in Alex, which did a good deal to recharge our batteries, we made the return desert train journey to Gambut. On reflection, what a pity that journey was never recorded on film, it would have made an epic "Great Train Journeys" episode. Upon our return to our unit we discovered that Flight Lieutenant Reid had been busy. I had mentioned to him of my interest in Air/Sea Rescue and consequently he had arranged a month's exchange posting with a launch wireless operator, the object being for us both to appreciate the conditions under which the other operated.

This was to prove the final twist in my combined operations type of war service. I had started as a trainee air gunner, spent almost three years at desert warfare and my final two years were to be spent with a naval unit but this time one dedicated to saving lives!

As soon as I reported for duty at the ASR base at Tobruk Harbour and saw those two sleek little vessels tied up at the jetty, I knew that this was the one for me! I was welcomed on board by the very friendly crew and found that I was a member of a ten-man team. There was the skipper the only commissioned officer, two NCO's, being the first and second coxswains, the LAC's consisting of two engine fitters and three deck hands plus the medical orderly and of course myself the wireless operator.

My first peep aboard convinced me that during my months stay I would be determined to do my utmost to get transferred to this branch of the service. I noticed that the small but tidy wireless cabin, the very heart of the vessel, was packed full of excellent equipment. The powerful transmitter/receiver was a Collins of American make, it was a beautiful little set to operate and far superior to our RAF equipment. There was a D/F set for passing bearings to the coxswain, VHF for the skipper's use on the bridge and IFF, a branch of radar. What a set-up, the wireless operator played a key role each time we put to sea.

A look around the engine room took my breath away! There were three beautifully polished 500hp Napier Lion aircraft engines, ingeniously converted to water-cooled marine engines. This hinted at the immense power bottled up in this small 63-foot vessel. My interest in small boats on the river Dee during the 20's and 30's sharpened my curiosity regarding the design of these launches. They were constructed entirely of timber, on the hard chine principle, having a smooth hull with a broad chine running the full length and around the stern. At high speed the vessel would lift out of the water and skimmed along on the chine giving greater buoyancy, less water resistance and so, far greater speed.

The famous speedboat ace, Scott Payne, had designed the Whalebacks, of which the two at Tobruk were an example. He was a senior RAF officer and had been helped with the whole concept and organisation of Air Sea Rescue in the early days by none other than Lawrence of Arabia. Enlisting as aircraftsman Shaw to preserve his anonymity he worked behind the scenes and was involved in quite important work. The main operational purpose of the Tobruk base was to provide cover for our 235 wing aircraft in the event of any of them ditching. They also covered the missions of the Beaufighter Squadrons who regularly carried out raids on the German held Greek islands, which could prove very demanding. Having hardly had time to settle in or become familiar with the set-up, I was informed that we were on duty boat and promptly received a call out signal. We were given a rendezvous position to cover a raid on the island of Kos and Leros, so all was set for my first ASR experience.

As the engines roared into life and we cast off, I realized that the very first problem confronting our coxswain was getting out of Tobruk. The harbour had, at that time, the unenviable record of being the most bomb-damaged area in the world. There were more than 140 chartered wrecks in the harbour as well as hundreds of small unmarked ones, so navigating through that lot to the open sea was a major task in itself. Once clear as we headed North West and the engines were turned up to the cruising speed of 1800revs, I began to realise what a beautiful vessel I was aboard. She just tore through the sea, and every member of the efficient crew knew his job, they worked like clockwork. It then dawned on me just how hard it would be for me to muscle-in on this branch of the service. They were all ex RNLI men, a very exclusive group; it was going to be difficult but I would do my best and maybe learn something from the experience.

The first lesson came very quickly and proved the logic of our C/O's idea of an exchange posting, "To experience the difficulties faced by launch operators" because as we raced through a *head-on* sea, the tiny wireless cabin was rising and falling with each wave. Occasionally (and you had to brace yourself for this) the cabin would rise a good 5 or 6 feet and then hit down again with a sickening crash! The old salts told me the reason was that generally speaking, every seventh wave was a big one and upon hitting these, the launch would virtually take off. Now I knew that nice flowing Morse was not a possibility when under way and explained why my set was facing stern with my back firmly seated towards the bows in order to absorb the shock!

Of all the crew, on this my initial voyage, my greatest admiration went to the engine fitters. Just one peep down the engine room hatch was enough for me; can you imagine the noise created by three aircraft engines, racing in an enclosed space? The two lads, fitted with earmuffs, were calmly checking valves, gauges and rev counters, as they nursed their beloved engines along. Despite all of this, for the 3 or 4-hour journey, the deck hands would be cheerfully occupied in the galley making tea or soup for everyone.

Once we reached our rendezvous, which was virtually in enemy waters, we hove to and had to remain in that position for the duration of the raid. I had to maintain a listening watch in case of any emergency and we remained there wallowing until finally, when all aircraft were accounted for, we received the return to base signal from Gambut. On our recall trip I again began to realise the power of the sea, for although we were travelling at some 30 knots, when the occasional big wave hit in a *following* sea, we would be pushed along and the sea would be controlling our actual speed. I also began to appreciate the brave band of men I was sharing this venture with. Each time they put to sea they were putting their lives at risk, not only with the hazard of the sea itself but also from enemy action. Their final aim was always to save lives, not to take it and I felt very proud to be involved with this branch of the RAF, whose motto was "The sea shall not have them", I prayed that I could become a part of it.

Home Comforts - chickens penned in a makeshift chicken coup, the fencing made with wire netting taken from transmitter

Me holding two oven ready chickens by the oven made from an old oil drum

Fred and me in our designer dug out in 1942

HMS Thunderbolt – the phoenix of Thetis

The launching of HMS Thetis

The Thetis disaster of 1938

Chapter 9

The Sea Shall not Have Them

On our return to Tubruk harbour fate was to take a hand in answering my prayer. As the coxswain was negotiating our way through the bomb-damaged litter, we unfortunately fouled one of the wrecks resulting in damage to our hull. I then had to contact our base in Alex to report the damage and request instructions. In the time honoured RAF procedure the instruction was that the skipper submits a detailed report, in triplicate, giving a full explanation of the accident and description of the damage. Having spotted my good handwriting in the signals log the skipper invited me into his cabin to write out the report as he dictated it to me. However before we commenced he asked, "Your accent sounds familiar, what part of "Blighty" do you come from?" When I replied, "Chester", it started a round of questions and answers, which I could not believe:

Skipper	What part of Chester?
Me	Well not exactly Chester, a little village called Mancot
Skipper	Oh yes, the village with the maternity home do you know it?
Me	Yes, I live just around the corner from there, my girlfriend works there.

Skipper	What did you do for a living?
Me	For a while, I worked at Bees Nursery.
Skipper	Do you know Mr Bully?
Me	Very well indeed, he is the owner.
Skipper	I live in Ness, he is my next-door neighbour.

It further transpired that our skipper, Flying Officer Nance, was the son of the farmer who owned the land adjacent to Ness Gardens, that he had been a member of the West Kirby Sailing Club and that the Second Coxswain, Corporal Gill, came from Morton on the Wirral and had been a member of the New Brighton Lifeboat crew. It took some time for such an amazing set of circumstances to sink in but it was the turning point for me. For the first time in my life I learned that "it is not so much <u>what</u> you know but <u>who</u> you know".

On completion of my spell with his crew, during which time I had taken part in several call outs, our skipper asked me, "Are you interested in joining ASR?" Upon receiving my positive response he asked me to deliver a letter to Flight Lieutenant Reid upon my return to my unit. The contents of that letter were to work like magic; good old "Nance" had pulled all the right strings for me, because within a few days, following my return, news came through that I had been posted to Air/Sea Rescue in Alexandria. To expedite things my C/O arranged for me to fly back to base on an aircraft of the Middle East Communications flight which called at Gambut daily to collect and deliver all official and confidential mail and packages.

The aircraft was an Avro Anson and once aboard I found that a crew of three was the usual limit. With the addition of myself plus kit, the plane was overloaded, so, to enable take off I was moved, together with the wireless operator, onto the main spa, which ran through the fuselage. Once airborne we returned to our normal positions of the wireless operator near the tail with his "set" and myself lying on the floor with my kit. The flight, in the normal course of events, would take something like two hours but once again things did not go quite to plan! Navigation with the old Anson was fairly elementary; we flew at a few hundred feet and simply followed the famous desert road to

Alex. About half an hour into the flight the inevitable sand storm blew up which resulted in the pilot having to fly even lower to pick out the road. When we were somewhere between Sidi Barrani and Mersa Matruh, the starboard engine suddenly started to splutter and then finally cut out. We had sand in the air intake! There was no way that we could make it on one engine but fortunately, at that very moment, the pilot spotted a small landing strip, close to the road. He thankfully put down there and not a moment too soon, as we landed the other engine packed in! Luck, however, was on our side; we had landed at a small RAF detachment, which boasted a couple of engine mechanics.

They offered us the hospitality of food and shelter until the storm blew out. The mechanics had fixed dust covers over our engines so the crew decided to stay the night. Our sleeping arrangements were on empty canteen tables, at least we were under cover and off the ground; we all slept soundly. First thing the next morning the lads cleaned up and serviced our engines and very soon we were on our way again. Without further mishap we landed safely at Alexandria. On my arrival at the Air/Sea Rescue base on the harbour, the ex KML Dutch shipping line terminal, I had to go through the usual RAF formality of being registered on the unit strength. Only then did I find out that I was posted to a launch at Bengazi! I had to go all the way back. No prizes for guessing my considered opinion of RAF organisation at that moment! My return journey, "up the blue" was to be via the hard and slow route, the desert road!

I was to travel on the Royal Navy mail truck, a weekly run delivering mail to naval detachments between Alex and Bengazi. For four torturous days I shared this run with the driver and what a run it proved to be! The surface of that notorious road was not only battle scarred and full of potholes but also red hot under the desert sun; this made it absolute murder on the tyres. After the first day we found that the rubber was simply melting and flying off in huge chunks. We constantly had to stop to change a wheel; this explained the large supply of wheels on board. I could not make up my mind whether all this was due to the conditions or the quality of the wartime rubber. During the trip we must have changed at least eight wheels. Fortunately for us, each night stop was at a naval unit where it seemed the driver was a familiar figure, so we were always well received. We were fed and accommodated under conditions where the sweat and toil of the day were soon forgotten.

Eventually, upon my arrival at Bengazi, I joined a rather well established ASR detachment, it was a two-boat base but here the crew had acquired a couple of very desirable residences! They were living in six-bed roomed luxury villas, which the owners had long since abandoned. By comparison to the lads in Tobruk the Bengazi lads lived in real luxury, only going to their launches when on duty boat or in the event of a call out. The call outs at Bengazi were few and far between because, unlike Tobruk, they did not cover any regular or specific operations. They were there simply to respond to any call for help from aircraft in their zone of activity, so I found life there, as in many units in wartime, was 90% boredom.

The launches at the Bengazi base were of a slightly newer version, still a product of Power Boat, Southhampton, but 68 footers with a much higher superstructure. These boats had been developed to give the skipper a far better range of vision; much better than they had in the old squat, and low-lying whaleback. However, the crews did not like them, saying that they were like double-decker buses and had nicknamed them "Hants and Dorsets".

During my tour of duty at this base I can only recall a couple of occasions when I was involved in a call out. It was during these that it began to dawn on me that most of our planet is covered in water because even when we reached the location of a distress call all that could be seen from a small vessel was mountains of water. We only knew that we were in the correct position thanks to the navigational skill of the coxswain and skipper. Once in position we would carry out an ever increasing square search, with every eye peeled for a sighting of an aircraft, dinghy or wreckage, as was quite often the rule, we found nothing. The frustration felt by ASR crews, whose sole wartime purpose was to save lives and being denied the opportunity to do so by the cruel sea, was unimaginable.

Just A Tick

Bengazi harbour had its fair share of air raids during the campaign, nothing like the intensity of Tubruk but still had a good number of sunken vessels to cause difficulties. Perhaps the most notorious was the remains of an ammunition ship, which had been hit near to the harbour entrance. The resulting explosion had ripped the vessel apart. The bows and stern had ended up so far apart that the navigable channel passed between them and these two portions of the ship were aptly referred to be the ASR crews as "William" and "Mary". During our long hours of duty boat we were all very busy keeping our vessel in ship-shape order. There was always lots of equipment to be maintained and one of the wireless operators duties entailed keeping the recognition markings on the foredeck freshly painted. A large area was painted yellow with red and white VHF squares, draughtboard style. These markings indicated to aircrew that we were a rescue craft with VHF for contact. Without these markings we could have been mistaken for a lone German E boat.

These distinctive markings were familiar to all of our squadrons and occasionally had been acknowledged by enemy aircraft, with no problems. The Americans with their "shoot first ask questions later" policy were spotting the fear we had. One of our launches had been attacked and lost, in a raid by one of the American formations who, on return to their base, had claimed to have sunk a German E boat. In the event of such a raid the only defence we had were two twin-Browning aircraft turrets, fore and aft.

Firing these from a platform bobbing up and down on the ocean was, to put it mildly, very difficult indeed. On many of our call outs we used to carry an extra deck cargo of 40-gallon drums of petrol. These were our reserve supply which on long trips had to pumped by hand into our main fuel tanks; hard work! The empty drums had to be sunk or they would form a deadly hazard to our small vessels. As they bobbed up and down on the waves they created very good gunnery practise. Enemy and friendly fire were not the only hazards we faced, the Mediterranean in wintertime can turn very ugly. Despite its reputation of being a "blue heaven" for holidaymakers, it can throw up some extremely violent storms in the winter. The New Testament refers to this in St Paul's account of his shipwrecking.

Our launches at Bengazi were numbered 2700 and 2701; we crewed 2700, and on one particular foul and stormy night our sister ship happened to be at sea in answer to an emergency call. On returning from yet another abortive voyage, as they approached the harbour entrance, the vessel was violently swept onto a reef and was eventually a total loss. The naval salvage party and we had a terrible struggle that night, getting the lads safely ashore by breeches buoy. During the next few weeks at high water and when the sea was calm, we managed to salvage most of the moveable equipment from the launch by ship's dinghy before finally leaving poor old 2701 to her fate.

Time and a fading memory do not permit me to recall the name of our skipper on 2700 but I do remember him as a real "old salt". An ex merchant seaman, my lasting memory of our skipper was of him chastising me for being a "land lubber"! The occasion related to our "cushy" shore billet where we had found that if you switched on a torch at night in the kitchen it was alive with cockroaches! To rectify the matter we had scrounged a drum of lime from the navy and had decided to decorate the room to rid it of the pests. We had salvaged some ladders and planks from a nearby-bombed building and I had volunteered to paint the <u>ceiling</u>. The skipper's sharp retort to this was "Deck Head lad, deck head!"

Eventually out tour of duty at Begazi came to an end, the relief launch arrived and we were instructed to return to base at Alexandria. This was a systematic procedure throughout the command, all launches had to be *slipped*[21] periodically for a complete overhaul and repainting. This was a time that all crews dreaded because suddenly, after being an intimate little team, working together and regardless of rank, calling each other by nicknames we became "Base Wallahs". This title was given to members of the large base unit where you were known by a number, housed in Barrack Blacks according to your rank and upon seeing an officer were expected to *throw-up* a salute; we hated it! The

---

21   This entailed being fitted in a cradle and hauled out of the water to dry

Just A Tick

idea of having this large pool of men was that when launches became available you would be called to crew them but not necessarily with your old "opos". No sooner had we settled into the base wallah period something came up on DRO's, which fired my imagination. It was an invitation for volunteers for a special operation.

At that period the Americans had mounted a very daring long-range raid on the Rumanian Oilfields, nothing of this nature had been attempted before. The Super Fortresses took off from Britain, carried out the raid and then carried on to land in the Middle East. One aircraft it seemed, had run out of fuel and made a forced landing in Turkey. Behind the scenes arrangements had apparently been made with the Turkish authorities to allow one of our vessels in to pick up the crew. This was to be an undercover job; the launch concerned was to be camouflaged as what we called a "banana boat". It would have a false bow and stern, mast and rigging to resemble a Greek fishing boat and the lads were all to be issued with civilian clothes. This sounded just what I was looking for and I duly volunteered.

The skipper selected for this special mission was the most cavalier of the unit, the hard-drinking, devil-may-care character – F/O Frankie Bottom. Frankie had such a reputation that many people in our own unit feared him. There is no doubt that he had his own crew lined-up for this operation but to make things appear more democratic, this call for volunteers was posted in the orderly room. When the launch was made ready for action all volunteers were summoned aboard for interview by Frankie and his coxswain. One of the first questions put to me was regarding my drinking habits and on being informed that I was tea-total a stroke was put through my name, and that was the end of my dream of adventure! Similar treatment was metered out to all volunteers who were not his original crewmembers; so much for democracy! Frankie's wireless operator, LAC Stockton, was a good friend of mine at base, a happy go lucky young lad who was loads of fun. When we eventually teamed up again Stocky told me in graphic detail all about that rescue mission but more of that later.

During my stay on base we witnessed some of the formality that went on there. On one occasion, as the old KML headquarters was adjacent to Ras El Tin, one of the royal Egyptian palaces, King Farouk was invited to the unit the purpose being a trip to sea in one of our launches. When he eventually arrived in one of his many Rolls Royce cars, his majesty was grandly dressed in a white uniform, as admiral of the Egyptian fleet! Amid much pomp and ceremony he took up his position on the bridge for the trip. However, the whole thing was just a publicity stunt as the press and photographers closely attended him. Fortunately we did not have to endure this kind of thing for long because quite soon, I was crewed up for another tour of duty; this time in HSL 167, another good old whaleback, with skipper Flying Officer Dunne, our destination Mersa Matruh.

Italian POW's Cooks

*Sailing in Mersa Matru harbour near the sunken
Italian Troop Ship Cita da Agrigento 1943*

Fishing in the lagoon

HSL 159 alongside at Mersa Matruh

HSL 159 at speed

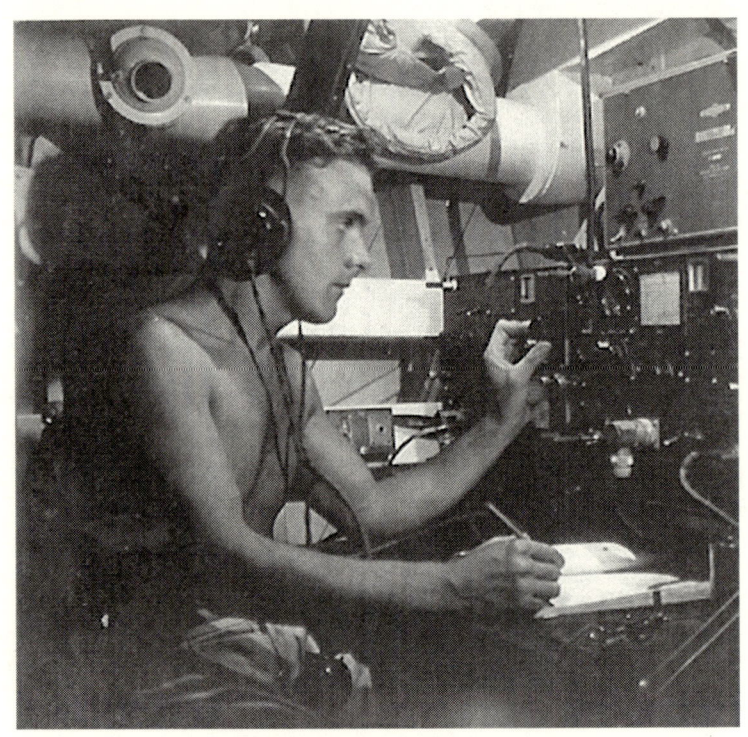

Me in Wireless Cabin HSL 159 1944

Me Testing Skippers VHF, Haifa 1944

Painting VHF squares on the foredeck

Me testing the gun turret of HSL 159

Chapter 10

Our Final Duty

My next tour of duty was to prove an absolutely amazing learning curve. Matruh, which for the last two years and during the desert campaign, had simply been a name on the map to us. It is a place on the Mediterranean coast, which we had always by-passed and was in fact a hidden gem just steeped in history. It was a tropical paradise and had for millennia been the secret holiday resort of the rich and famous. When we arrived and took over the base from the departing, time expired launch crew, we found that we had this tropical haven to ourselves. Matruh had been a hive of naval activity but was now deserted as the campaign had moved along the coast in preparation for the invasion of Italy; we were simply providing air/sea rescue cover for this section of the coast. Ours was a one-boat base, call outs were few and far between and as we ten were the only military personnel we had lots of time to enjoy our slice of paradise and study local history.

The first thing that we discovered was that Matruh was built overlooking a magnificent shallow blue lagoon, edged by white sandy beaches, totally protected from the sea by a beautiful reef. The entrance to the lagoon was by a small gap in the reef and buoys marked the navigable channel to a small jetty, this was our base. The most amazing sight however, was that in the centre of the lagoon lay a partially sunken Italian liner, the "Cita da Agrigento", probably 15,000 tons, she lay on her port beam. She had apparently been brought into this safe haven during Rommel's advance to El Alemean when the Germans and Italians confidently believed that Egypt was conquered. They believed that the lagoon was protected from attack be the reef but they had reckoned without the fleet air arm who had sent in a flight of torpedo carrying aircraft. This had flown in low over the reef and struck the "Cita da Agrigento" a mortal blow; she would not put to sea again and for our stay was our war prize.

No sooner had we established ourselves than we found we had a regular visitor and companion in Maadi, a very friendly old fisherman who worked from our jetty. He made quite a good living by fishing the lagoon and selling his catch locally; this old character proved to be a veritable hive of information regarding local history. Back in the times of ancient Egypt, the old man told us, this lagoon had been developed as a holiday resort and during the Roman period, a magnificent villa had been built on the overlooking hillside. This, he said, had been the secret love nest of Mark Anthony and Cleopatra! In the 1930's the Egyptian government had built a very grand hotel on the same site and during the 1940's it was still functional and being used by our forces as an officers mess. However, his most astounding piece of information was that the hotel played host, prior to his abdication, to King Edward VIII and Mrs Simpson whilst on one of their mystery Mediterranean cruises; could they have chosen a more romantic location?

One eventful day the old man rowed a group of us across the lagoon and studying the bottom through crystal clear water was magical. Just like the Great Barrier Reef, this reef was rich in natural sponges and before the days of synthetics a prosperous trade in that commodity had flourished here. When we landed on the edge of the reef we found it riddled with small caves but the cave that the old fisherman wanted us to see had openings both to the lagoon and to the sea. At high tide the waves could flush right the way through with the result being a deposit of beautiful white sand on the cave floor. The most amazing feature of this cave was that in its centre the sea had hollowed out a large basin, which was filled with crystal clear, cool water. We all enjoyed a dip as the old man told us that the water was changed at every high tide and that what we were all bathing in was Cleopatra's pool. He said that the queen had bathed in this secluded, private place, protected from the burning sun. What a wonderful story, and one we simply had to believe! Since that time I have often wondered, were the King and Mrs Simpson as fortunate as we lads in having shared Cleopatra's bath chamber?

As I previously mentioned, the "Cita da Agrigento" was to prove quite a prize for us with many rich pickings in the way of fittings and equipment and with her help we were able to constantly improve our base. Almost daily we would row across the lagoon to the wreck in the ship's dinghy and bring over any moveable items that would make life easier and more comfortable. We had been allocated two Italian prisoners of war, Toni and Nino, to act as cooks; they were invaluable members of our unit bringing our number to twelve. For sleeping arrangements we now had a tented area ashore and with the timber, panels etc. that we salvaged from the wreck we had built quite an impressive base, giving us living quarters independent of the launch.

Our first construction was an excellent cookhouse, well equipped with fittings from the wrecked ship's galley, Toni and Nino were delighted and proved to be excellent cooks. The next to be built was our cosy dining room with some very comfortable tables and chairs, this was followed by the construction of a games room complete with a table tennis facilities and a darts board. The final building however was our touch of luxury – a tiled bathhouse, complete with a slipper bath and shower, all acquired from the wrecked ship's captain's quarters! We were indeed living the life of riley.

Meanwhile, back home, Bomber Harris was now mounting his 1000 bomber raids on German cities; this was in reprisal to Germany's blitz on Britain. Reports indicated that the losses of RAF aircrew were appalling and it appeared that the service were now scraping the bottom of the barrel for replacements because suddenly a signal arrived the gist of which was me being posted back to the UK for flying duties.

Studying the signal, the skipper said, "Leave this one with me" and his subsequent reply must have indicated to the powers that be that I could not be spared from the vital air/sea rescue service! He certainly must have pulled all of the right strings because we heard no more and I continued to lead my worm's eye view existence, all be it from sea level!

It was about this time that we came to realise that as the eighth army had moved out of their territory, the Egyptians were making plans for a return to normality. One day, as we were returning to harbour following a trip out to sea for engine testing, we were greeted on the jetty by a smartly dressed British Army officer, who proved to be the British Commissioner employed by the Egyptian government to reinstate Matruh to its former peaceful role. He had spotted us speeding across the lagoon and asked whether he could come aboard for a trip out. We of course welcomed him and invited him to join us but unfortunately as he attempted to jump aboard, he missed his footing and ended up in the *drink*! We fished him out, dried his clothes, gave him a hot drink and before long the poor man's humiliation evaporated and he was all smiles. From that moment we all became firm friends and whenever we had a test run planned he and his wife would join us and in return we were often invited up to their hillside villa.

Whenever we entertained the commissioner and his wife we were proud to show off our very comfortable base and explained how and where we had acquired all the luxury fixtures and fittings. The commissioner, of course, had his duties to fulfil and being a member of the Egyptian civil service, the one thing that he knew very well was that the "Cita da Agrigento" was now the property of the Egyptian government. He obviously filed a report regarding our activities regarding the wreck as quite soon we received a signal from base forbidding us to board the wrecked vessel. We did keep in touch with the commissioner after that but the relationship was never the same. With the approach of winter 1944 we began to experience worsening weather conditions with fierce storms, reminiscent of our Bengazi days. It was one of these storms that finally brought our Mersa Matruh tour to an end.

It came about that late one night during a particularly violent gale; we received a distress call from a Baltimore aircraft that was out on convoy patrol. The signal intimated that they had engine trouble and that they were just about to ditch just off our section of the coast. In response we dashed down the channel and across the lagoon and as we were going through the break in the reef to the open stormy sea the skipper shouted, "Full speed ahead". This command was to prove fatal for as we hit the first giant wave the launch literally leapt out of the water, coming down again with such a sickening crash and the coxswain knew immediately that she had broken her back! Not being able to continue under such appalling conditions we had to reluctantly call off the mission. We limped back to the lagoon leaving the poor aircraft crew to their fate; the probability was however that the savage sea that had wrecked our vessel would have given them very little chance of survival.

We now received orders that as soon as our relief launch arrived and weather permitting, we were to proceed in our vessel to headquarters in Alexandria to undergo a hull survey (the vessel eventually proved to be a write off). With the final arrival of the relief launch can you imagine my delight at discovering that the wireless operator was non other than my good friend "Stocky". He had returned from his Turkish operation and along with his Greek fishermen mates had been allocated this other launch. They had been sent over to Matruh for a well-earned break and from Stocky I now learned details of the hazardous undertaking in which they were involved, an operation for which Flying Officer Frank Bottom had received the OBE. As the weather was still somewhat stormy, it was deemed unadvisable to attempt sailing our crippled vessel back to Alex, so we enjoyed sharing Matruh with this happy-go-lucky bunch of lads for a further week.

Stocky shared my tent and as we lay on our beds relaxing on the first day of our reunion, he recounted to me the following details of their Turkish operation:

"When work was completed our fully disguised launch really did look like a Greek fishing boat, with a false superstructure, gunwales and high bow and stern. We were togged out in scruffy old civvies and our first job was to load as much deck cargo fuel, in 40 gallon drums, as possible but this had to be concealed to save giving the game away. Once prepared we cast off and set sail for Turkey.

The first leg of the journey was achieved at normal speed but as we approached the Turkish coast we had to just idle along, masquerading as local fishermen. The hard part was going to be negotiating the narrow strait between Rhodes and Turkey because at that time the German forces occupied Rhodes. One very humorous incident occurred when we were progressing nicely and hugging the Turkish coast. We must have been travelling a little too fast as we aroused the suspicions of a party of Turkish troops on coastal patrol and suddenly we came under intense rifle fire from the top of a cliff. Quickly showing his cavalier spirit, Frankie hoisted the RAF ensign and shouted to them over the load hailer, "Stop firing you stupid b……s, can't you see we are British!?" Miraculously the firing immediately ceased! We made it safely to the point where American airmen were waiting and while Frankie went ashore to negotiate their release we all worked hard transferring the deck cargo of petrol into the main tanks; this was extremely hard work using hand pumps in which we all took turns.

It was of course well known that during the war Turkey was riddled with spies (from both sides) and it was almost certain that all of our activity was well noted by the German element. This was proved later that night as we tried to slip quietly through the straight to head back when we were picked up by searchlight and challenged. When we did not respond the Germans sent out an E boat to "bring us in". The E boat was reputed to be the fastest in service, capable of outrunning any vessel and as they picked us out in their searchlight they fired a shot across our bows and we knew the game of bluff was over. We were wondering what our fate would be if we were captured in civilian clothes when suddenly Frankie shouted to the engine room over the ship's intercom, "Right lads, full speed ahead". Now good old HSL159 showed the Germans what she had been built for – speed! At 2,200 revolutions maximum we presented a clean pair of heels to the pursuing Germans and although they straddled us with some shellfire, after half an hour of hard running we managed to shake them off.

Just A Tick

We gained the open sea and the frustrated enemy gave up the chase. By first light we were all relieved to find no further sign of enemy activity so we set course for Alex at normal cruising speed. However, by midday we discovered that the chase had played havoc with our fuel supply, which was running dangerously low. Come late afternoon, despite all attempts at economising, we had completely run out of petrol, the tanks were dry. Even more worrying was the fact that a couple of futile attempts to restart the engines had completely flattened the ship's batteries. We were now dead in the water with no power, there was no way to contact Alex to alert them of our plight or position. If the Germans had sent out a plane to track us down we were now sitting ducks! Not to be outdone Frankie once again showed his determination and ingenuity. Getting together all the canvas sheets and tarpaulins we had on board he rigged up some temporary sails. As the sails filled out we set course again for Alex, only now with a top speed of about 3 knots.

By this time the American lads, who admitted to not being very good sailors, were feeling very sick due to the movement of the boat. They were also very depressed and voiced their fears that we were never going to see dry land again. After a couple of days of this wallowing and with rations running low everyone began to get a little apprehensive. Frankie would have none of it, we were on course for Alex, he said and if it took us a week we would still get back. More worrying for him and his merry men though was the fact that not only had we run out of petrol but the beer supply had also dried up!

One morning, following a further three days of this tortuous progress we were all excited to see a small dot in the sky. This turned out to be a search aircraft sent out by a worried command to look for us. Circling above, he gave a reassuring wiggle of his wings and before long we had a rescue launch alongside. They secured lines to our bows and towed us back to Alex harbour and our base, much to the relief of all concerned. In particular, the American lads showed their relief as they jumped ashore as soon as we tied up, and then proceeded to kiss the ground.

With a little bit of clever manoeuvring we were able to return and prolong our stay at Matruh with this happy-go-lucky, devil-may-care and courageous bunch of lads. The following couple of weeks were probably the most relaxed and enjoyable of all my wartime service in the RAF. Although the weather had improved considerably and conditions were ideal for our trip back to Alex, the skipper kept sending signals back to base advising caution regarding the sea worthiness of 167. These warnings were really quite groundless as the launch was seaworthy but base were not to know this and in the meantime we could carry on enjoying our time at Matruh. We had also struck-up an association with an American air force unit based on the Matruh landing ground they were a really mad crowd but good company. Whenever they decided to pay us a visit their fleet of jeeps would arrive in a cloud of dust, with all the guys riding cowboy style, shouting "Yippee" and waving their hats. Whenever they arrived we were assured a couple of hilarious hours.

This carefree time can probably be summed up by one little episode I so clearly remember. We were informed that an ENSA party had arrived at the landing ground and would be giving a concert in one of our derelict and disused hangers. This sad and rusty old building was really ready for demolition but had been hastily converted into a makeshift concert hall. On the evening of the concert the old hanger was bursting at the seams with troops from the surrounding areas. The ENSA party were being given a rousing reception, especially when any of the female artists appeared on the stage. Suddenly, the whole evening turned into a state of chaotic farce and comedy as one artist, a baritone soloist, took to the stage and the piano struck up with the familiar introduction to a well-known sentimental song. This song was very popular at the time with most music hall artists but as the hush descended over the audience, quite suddenly and loudly Stocky shouted out, "Oh no! Not Bless This Bloody House!". I need hardly tell you that cry literally brought the house down, everyone including the ENSA party were howling with laughter, even the baritone as he performed his "party piece", had a job to keep a straight face.

Such then was our association with a great set of lads who epitomized the sense of humour that prevailed in the armed forces during the war years. Enabling us to overcome all obstacles, these men were head and shoulders above the rest of us. So it was with great reluctance that we eventually had to say our farewells, cast-off and set sail for Alex. Sadly, I never again encountered Stocky or his mates.

Jock Black and me, with Cleopatra on leave in Alexandria

Chapter 11

Goodbye Air/Sea Men

So, for us, it was back to the Big Base with its barrack room existence. The brief period that we all dreaded as it meant an end, temporarily, to the spirit of comradeship that we had all shared at the small detached bases. Our poor old launch was slipped and after survey, found to have broken her back. She was condemned, to be broken up, a sad moment for us all. It was now a waiting game for the next launch to come off the slip, be re-commissioned and await the next crew.

It was during that period of waiting that we once again encountered the sense of humour that prevailed in the service. Alex, at that time was overrun with hundreds of locals seeking employment; unfortunately the majority were bone-idle and were seeking handouts rather than work. The odd one would prove to be a really good reliable worker and once found you would hang on to him and issue him with an official pass, which he would proudly display. These passes were of great value to them whenever they boarded one of the dozens of ships, anchored in the large harbour, seeking work. Of course the lads who staffed our Orderly room who issued these passes were constantly being plagued for a pass by the unemployable element. For a bit of fun they came up with the idea of issuing "fake" passes. These really did look like the real thing, with RAF unit stamps and elaborate signatures, however when we saw the prototype in our barrack room imagine the response at the actual content of the pass:

> To whom it may concern
>
> ABDUL EL GAZOOZ
>
> Was employed by this unit for a very short period. During that time we found him to be the most idle and stupid git imaginable. If he boards your ship looking for work please do me a favour:
>
> KICK HIS ARSE OVERBOARD
>
> Signed   *Joe Bloggs*
>   Squadron Leader

I do not know whether any Ship's Officer ever carried out the instruction to the letter but I will wager they had many a chuckle over these fakes. For sure, the holder of such a pass would not be greatly helped in his search for employment!

My wait at Alex, on this occasion, was quite a short one because very soon the next launch came off the slipway, all spick and span and to my delight I was drafted to her as wireless operator. Unfortunately, none of my old crew buddies from Matruh were included; it was a totally different crew with Skipper F/LT Forster. How pleased we all were to discover that we were to serve HSL159, the famous launch, and fresh from her Turkish rescue trip. Now of course she had the camouflage removed as she was back on normal rescue duties. We had now entered the year of 1945, later to be the final year of the war; Hitler was constantly threatening the use of his "secret weapon" and as everyone knew what that threat constituted, all units were kept on their toes. Our next tour of duty in 159 was to cover the Levant area, the coastline of The Lebanon and Palestine; we were to be based at Haifa.

Once established in the harbour, we found that our activities were to be quite limited. We came under the direct control of the Royal Navy and were more or less restricted to shore patrols. Most of our time was spent in keeping our vessel "ship-shape" and doing exercise runs to keep the engines in tip-top condition. Call-outs to aircraft in distress were now virtually non-existent and the only rescue operation I can recall us having to perform was when we received a distress signal from a small launch. This vessel carried a party of Marine Commandos who had carried out a secret raid on the Island of Crete, then in German hands. During its return while still far out at sea, it had developed engine trouble, they were in a similar situation to the one 159 had been in following her Turkish episode, so now it was our turn to help out.

When we finally located them, much to their relief, we secured lines to their bows and towed them quickly back to their base at Beirut. Just for devilment, Skipper Forster decided to give these guys a bit of a thrill and ordered the engine room to "open up". Imagine the scene as we tore across the Med in a cloud of spray, with the raiding party hanging on for dear life as they bounced along on our wake. We soon had them back in harbour and as we tied up the breathless commandos came to shake hands and thank us for getting them back safely. As they voiced their thanks they said how amazed they were at our launch's performance and that they had never travelled so fast across the sea in their lives.

It was at this time that another episode occurred to demonstrate what a small world it is. In one of her letters my girlfriend Dot informed me that a family friend, school chum and former neighbour from Liverpool, George Chesterman, was a constable in the Palestine Police force and was stationed at Kiriat Hein, near Acre. I quickly got in touch with George and subsequently we paid each other many visits. He would come down to Haifa with us during test runs and he would invite me to their police station. He would greatly enjoy his trips out to sea and likewise I would enjoy the many conducted tours he gave me of the ancient Crusader fortifications of Acre. Amazingly these fortifications were still in perfect condition and occupied. Acre is the place where Edward I would have landed during his participation in the Crusades and it was those fortification structures that he copied for his ring of castles in North Wales.

During this period of duty we had ample time and opportunity to explore many of the places of interest in the Holy Land. This included Caesarea, The Dead Sea and the Sea of Galilee but everywhere we travelled we detected an undertone. The hatred between Jew and Arab was very evident and it seemed at that time the only stabilising force was the Palestine Police. They of course had both Jewish and Arab recruits and did maintain a good degree of law and order and there is no doubt that without their control over civil affairs, complete chaos would have resulted. Thanks to my contact with George and his comrades I was able to get a good insight into this very complex country. For their part the Jews claimed Palestine as their "Promised Land", which was given by God to Moses; on the other hand, the Muslims claimed it as their historic homeland long before the arrival of their prophet Mohamed. During the 20th century and the First World War however, the British government had really upset the balance. In order to get the Arab tribes, along with Lawrence of Arabia, to fight a gorilla type war against the Turks they (the British Government via Lawrence) had given their assurance that after hostilities Palestine would become an independent Arab state. However, when the Turks were finally defeated the British government went back on their word, much to the frustration of Lawrence, they issued the Balfour Declaration promising the land, Israel, to the Jews.

This "double-cross" infuriated the Arab world, turning them into Britain's bitter enemies but at the same time they also inflamed the Jews by only allowing a strictly controlled, small number of immigrants into the country each year. So, this hornet's nest was the Holy Land, administered as a British mandate under the League of Nations. In reality, law and order was being enforced by the Palestine Police, on military lines and theirs was an unenviable job, being seen by both sides with hatred and regarded as an occupying force. It was now September 1945 and one bright sunny day as we were all about our daily duties, keeping our beloved 159 in good shape, we received a signal: "**Tomorrow you will dress ship, it is VE day**". This came as something of a shock, all our duties would cease as **WE WERE AT PEACE.**

Next morning, Skipper Forster addressed us: "Best KD today lads, let us all go up to the railway sidings to greet the first trainload of survivors from Buchenwald". It seemed now international pressure was on Britain to allow unlimited members of these survivors into Palestine but unknown to us the Royal Navy had intercepted and turned away several ships heading for Haifa. We all duly lined up, in smart order, awaiting the arrival of the train. As at last the train drew in to the station we were shocked to see that the poor unfortunate and wretched human beings were being transported in cattle trucks! They looked dreadful; we were expecting smiles and cheers as they arrived at their "Promised Land" but instead we were confronted with utter silence and sullen stares from them. Suddenly, they all started spitting at us as they hurled abuse in languages we could not understand. In disbelief, I said to Skipper Forster, "What is all that about, Sir?" his quiet reply was: "We have done our bit lads, what we see now is beyond our control". No doubt we had encountered the founder members of the Stern Gang and Haganah[22] and with the final withdrawal of British forces from Palestine the blood bath, in that most unholy of lands, was about to begin.

There is no doubt that any branch of humanity, which is founded on violence, should take note of the old biblical quote from the prophet Hosea, "If you sow the wind you must reap the whirlwind".

---

22   The first Jewish terror gangs or freedom fighters

And Finally

When I look back on a very long and eventful lifetime, I am amazed that the first 25 years are deeply embedded in my mind and can be recalled with such vivid clarity. The following 64 years are worthy of at least two more books as during that time Dot and I raised a large and very loving family. Each and every one was a gem and I think that they have all grown up to be good citizens despite the fact that we were not able to lavish them with many material things. We gave them all the love, affection and attention possible, which I think are the basic needs of any child.

As a preamble to this book, I feel that it is appropriate to mention all offspring, from the family that Dot and I reared.

1947 – Patricia Eileen who married Keith Vickers and produced
    2 Grandchildren, Alexander Lee and Sian Elen
        Lee married Cheryl Fisher and produced
            2 Great grandchildren, Alexander Ioan and Aled Iorwerth

1948 – Alan John married Rose Jackson and produced
    2 Grandchildren, Mark and Wendy
        Mark married Laura and produced
            2 Great grandchildren, Adam and Johnathan

Wendy who married and produced
3 Great grandchildren, Lean, Sophie and Jemma

1950 – Robert Joseph who married Susan Mottram and produced
2 Grandchildren, Alexander and Joanne
Alexander and his partner Alex Kirk produced
1 Great grandchild, Joshua
Joanne married Alistaire Gardiner and produced
2 Great grandchildren, Victoria and Elizabeth

1953 – Geraint James who married Frances Jones and produced
2 Grandchildren, Gareth and Rhys

1955 – Gaenor Caroline who married John Hughes and produced
2 Grandchildren, Darryl and Carey
Darryl married Verity and produced
1 Great grandchild, Jorja
(Gaenor and her offspring now live in New Zealand and Gaenor is married to New Zealander, Richard Hunter)

1961 – Christina Gwendoline (Nina) who married Anthony Ainsbury and produced
3 Grandchildren, Jennifer, Paul and Martin

1963 – Jaqueline Norma who married Ralf Detlefsen and produced
1 Grandchild, Emma Sofia
(Jaquie and her family also live in New Zealand)

1966 – Amanda Jane who married John Thomas and produced
2 Grandchildren, Luke and Joel

I have no doubt that before I pass on there will be many more additions to the family; I live in the hope of seeing great-great grandchildren!

LaVergne, TN USA
09 November 2010

204190LV00001B/144/P